T0197220

YOUR HEALTHY FUTURE

LIVING ABOVE THE FREQUENCY OF DISEASE

MARIA B. BARNES

BALBOA.PRESS

A DIVISION OF HAY HOUSE

Balboa Press books may be ordered through booksellers or by contacting:

Balboa Press
A Division of Hay House
1663 Liberty Drive
Bloomington, IN 47403
www.balboapress.com
844-682-1282

Because of the dynamic nature of the Internet, any web addresses or links contained in this book may have changed since publication and may no longer be valid. The views expressed in this work are solely those of the author and do not necessarily reflect the views of the publisher, and the publisher hereby disclaims any responsibility for them.

The author of this book does not dispense medical advice or prescribe the use of any technique as a form of treatment for physical, emotional, or medical problems without the advice of a physician, either directly or indirectly. The intent of the author is only to offer information of a general nature to help you in your quest for emotional and spiritual well-being. In the event you use any of the information in this book for yourself, which is your constitutional right, the author and the publisher assume no responsibility for your actions.

Cover Design: Jennifer Stimson
Editing: Trever McKenzie
Author Photo Credit: Valerie Bey/Valerie Bey Photography

Print information available on the last page.

ISBN: 978-1-9822-6928-9 (sc)
ISBN: 978-1-9822-6927-2 (hc)
ISBN: 978-1-9822-6926-5 (e)

Library of Congress Control Number: 2021910286

Balboa Press rev. date: 05/25/2021

CONTENTS

For Kevin, my heart's delight.

CHAPTER 1

LIVING IN FEAR OF DISEASE

"Why am I so afraid of getting sick?" It wasn't the first time that Allison asked herself that question, and she knew it wouldn't be the last. With her meeting about to begin, she finished drying her hands, checked her makeup and hair in the restroom mirror, and returned to the conference room, where the team leads were assembling. As the head of Human Resources, Allison was in charge of her firm's Employee Wellness Campaign. She had spent a lot of time overseeing the details of the project and was pleased it was almost ready to roll out. As she entered the room, Allison greeted her staff and settled in to review several outstanding issues.

In her early thirties, with a thriving career, a marriage to the man of her dreams, and a life in a well-to-do suburb of Cincinnati, Ohio, Allison seemed to have it all. For that, she was grateful. Yet despite her good fortune and the fact that she had rarely been sick a day in her life, somewhere in the back of her mind, she had to admit that she was waiting for the proverbial shoe to drop.

Her own mother died of ovarian cancer when she was just

fifteen, leaving her dad to raise her and her little brother. That loss left her reeling for years. Deep inside, she felt she could have done more, should have been more loving, and would have been a better daughter if only she knew how short life with her mother was destined to be. Over time, the guilt led her to become overly concerned about her family – in particular, her dad. She found herself constantly panicked about his well-being, and she lived in perpetual fear that disaster would strike again.

After high school, Allison opted to commute to the University of Cincinnati and live at home rather than attend an out-of-state school. She worked hard to stay focused, concentrated on getting good grades, and graduated with honors. She met Mike soon after college, and several years later, the two got married and bought a home in her old neighborhood. Although her brother went to college on the West Coast and now lived in Chicago, Allison remained tied to her hometown and spent a lot of time with both her dad and Mike's parents.

To her friends, she seemed well adjusted and happy. Her coworkers liked and respected her. But behind her friendly façade, her worries were intensifying. Why? Because she knew that no matter what, bad things happen to the best of people. The news that her cousin had multiple sclerosis (MS) and that her father developed a heart condition did nothing to calm her fears. Her panic attacks returned. She was not only afraid for her father, but deeply concerned about the state of her own health.

Her world was beginning to crumble and she felt powerless to do anything about it. Every call from her dad made her heart beat a little faster as she waited for the bad news she believed was bound to follow. With every ache or pain, she began to worry that she, too, would develop a chronic disease and die early, like her mom did. Increasingly, she found herself waking up in the middle of the night, wondering what lay ahead.

That night was no different. She and Mike turned out the lights at 10:00 p.m. But several hours later, there she was: wide

Maria B. Barnes

awake, staring at the ceiling fan, reviewing all the details of the day, and worrying about the pain that cropped up in the middle of her back. She decided to schedule an X-ray during her next visit to the chiropractor and turned over to check that Mike was still breathing. With all of her insecurities bubbling up, she was fearful of losing him and had a hard time envisioning him safe and sound as he went about his day.

She knew she should be more like her husband: fun-loving and fearless. She loved his carefree approach to life and curiosity. But they were, in many ways, complete opposites. Mike was outdoorsy; she was not. He was into off-road biking; she was afraid to get on a bicycle. He enjoyed adventure, thrived on risk, and loved the possibilities presented by the unknown. She planned everything down to a T and worried that nothing was ever good enough. As he began to expand his world, she knew her efforts to stay safe were beginning to limit her in a way that could eventually impact her marriage. Already, her recently developed fear of flying threw a wrench into their plans for a vacation in Hawaii.

The next afternoon, Allison sat at her desk, ostensibly reviewing agreed-on changes to the campaign while watching large, white clouds move energetically across a brilliant blue sky. She stood up and walked over to the window, deep in thought as red and gold leaves tumbled by on a burst of wind. She was worried about what the X-ray of her spine would reveal. Despite how light and beautiful the outside world was, Allison knew that her inner world was descending into darkness. She wanted to be excited about life. She wanted to relax. More than anything, she wanted to quit worrying about her health. But she just could not find a way to let her guard down.

The older she got, the more she tried to solve her problem by popping pills. It began with vitamins, moved on to antacids, and was now prescriptive drugs for her panic attacks. With germs and disease all around, and the people in her life getting sick and potentially dying, Allison had to admit that she was crippled by fear. As she tried to calm herself down, she wondered, "Will I ever stop being afraid of life, afraid of getting sick? Please, God! Just let me know I'm going to be okay!" With that, she made a promise to herself to find a way to stop being afraid of death and disease.

CHAPTER 2

MY CANCER JOURNEY

My journey with cancer has been a long one. It began in my mid-forties, when I was diagnosed with breast cancer. Roughly ten years later, I received the diagnosis of Stage 4 metastatic breast cancer. Today, however, I am in complete remission, living a healthy, vibrant life. This should tell you two things: number one, I am no stranger to fear and disease; and number two, it *is* possible to overcome any fear and be cured from a deadly illness.

Unfortunately, for thousands of breast cancer survivors, the rate of disease recurrence is roughly 30 percent, regardless of any treatment a survivor chooses to undergo. That is why I do not believe my journey is anything out of the ordinary until we get to the part about remission.

Metastatic breast cancer is, according to the medical community, incurable. When I sat down with my oncologist after my second diagnosis and listened to her tell me that she could extend my life but not cure me, somewhere in the back of my mind, I decided not to accept her prediction for my future. In that moment, I began to tell myself a different story. I remember thinking I would be okay and that I would not die from the disease. I knew I had no idea how that would happen, but I had faith. Looking back, I now know I was silently acknowledging that I am an extremely powerful being and that my life can be whatever I choose it to be.

The truth is you have the power to avoid all illnesses. You also have the power to cure yourself from any disease. Unfortunately, most of us were never told that; in fact, we have been programmed to believe the exact opposite. In all the time I spent in and out of doctors' offices and hospitals, no one ever suggested any option for treatment outside of what I received. If I wanted anything different, I was on my own.

The gift in all of this is that if you can accept that fear is disease and disease is a manifestation of fear, you can set out to turn that around and stop believing a pill or a vaccine will save you. As I learned, that is a powerful and necessary belief. There comes a point where traditional Western medicine has no more answers for you. It can only go so far when it comes to treating chronic and terminal disease. To keep going further, you must find a way to "step it up" for yourself.

It begins by addressing fear head on. From where you are today, how do you view fear? Hopefully, as a wakeup call and a big "note to self." By paying attention and answering the call that your body, mind, and soul are broadcasting, you can change lanes and put yourself on a completely new path – one that is happy, healthy, and fearless. The bottom line is that you *can* put fear behind you. You just need to know how.

My Early Fears

Over the course of my journey with cancer, I took a trip down Memory Lane to pinpoint when I first remember being fearful of getting sick or dying. It was the death of my grandfather on Halloween night when I was nine years old. My father was away on business, and my mother took us to a party at a friend's house. Everyone had a wonderful time that evening, and we returned home in an upbeat, energetic mood.

But at some point in the middle of the night, I woke up with a feeling of complete dread. Something was terribly wrong. As I lay in my bed wondering why I was feeling so strange, I heard the telephone ring. I got up and opened my bedroom door. Across the hallway in her bedroom, I could hear my mother speaking in a sad, heavy voice. I stood completely still, unsure of what to do. When she hung up, I heard her burst into tears. I ran into my parents' bedroom, where I saw she had flung herself across the bed, crying her eyes out into a pillow.

I was terrified to hear any bad news but needed to know what had happened that had left her so devastated. I blurted out, "Mommy, what's wrong?!" She turned slightly and sobbed, "Daddy's dead!" In that instant, my entire body froze. I was petrified by the thought that my father was dead. "My daddy?" I managed to choke out. "No, *my* daddy!" she wailed. A wave of extreme relief ran through me, followed quickly by an overwhelming feeling of great distress, shock and utter sadness. My mother continued to cry so loudly and deeply that I was at a complete loss. I had never witnessed such grief. Not knowing how to comfort her, I turned and went back to my room, where I curled up in my bed and shivered involuntarily for what seemed like hours.

Fast-forward ten years. All of my grandparents had died, either from cancer or heart disease. I had also lost a few friends in car accidents. When I was thirty-two, my best friend from first and second grade died from metastatic breast cancer. By the time I was forty, both my sister and mother were surviving breast cancer, and a brother had recovered from skin cancer.

All of this certainly gave me pause. But was I consciously afraid of getting sick myself and possibly dying? No. As difficult as it all was, I did not believe I was living in fear or that I would get cancer. However, I want to stop here and point out that fear comes in many forms. The one that was front and center in my life was stress.

By the time I was forty-five, the stress of my career was exhausting me. As fun as a career in video was, it required extreme attention to detail, the ability to meet tight deadlines, and a lot of travel. I was getting up every morning, having a multi-shot cappuccino for breakfast, and running the entire day on adrenaline. I wondered why my body wanted to go back to bed after breakfast and just pushed myself harder. My attention was so focused outside of myself that I missed my body's internal warning signs. It all came to a head on a sunny afternoon in Portugal.

My First Diagnosis

It was the summer of 2006, and my husband and I were vacationing in Lisbon. He lived there for four years as a teen, and we were back so that he could attend his high school reunion and catch up with a few of his former classmates. One afternoon, in between the planned activities, we drove up the coast to Sintra, where we took a tour of the Romanticist castle, known as the Pena Palace, and had a wonderful lunch in a nearby café. The outing could not have been any nicer or the weather more pleasant, and I was feeling great.

But between the time we began the drive back down the coast and our arrival at the hotel, I became so sick that I could hardly sit upright. It felt like a heavy theater curtain collapsed over my entire body and was suffocating me. I managed to get up to the room and lie down, realizing that I had never felt so sick in my entire life. It was like the flu times ten.

For the rest of our stay in Portugal, I managed to get up and about with the help of over-the-counter medications from the local pharmacy. Clearly, something was wrong. What began as a delightful summer trip was ending in disaster and by the end of the week, I was still very sick. I knew I needed to see a doctor, but the last thing I wanted to do was end up in a hospital overseas. The night before we flew back to the U.S., as I went in and out of consciousness, I felt a lump in my right breast and knew immediately what it was. Was I scared? No. I was too sick to care. The next day, we boarded the flight and headed home, where several days later, I was diagnosed with pneumonia and Stage 2 breast cancer.

After recovering from the pneumonia, I began my cancer treatment at Georgetown University's Lombardy Cancer Center in Washington, DC. The regimen included undergoing a lumpectomy of the right breast, months of chemotherapy, and six weeks of radiation. The chemo was difficult and the side effects too numerous to count. But I made it through with flying colors, working the entire time. I took a day off for each chemo infusion and returned to the office the day after. All I wanted was to have my old life back.

But try as I might, that proved to be difficult because my world changed. My body was different, my brain was different due to the chemotherapy, and everything seemed extremely temporary. As a result, nothing seemed worth doing. It became a strange experience of walking through my life with true detachment. Was it fear? I cannot say. What was clear is that I needed to focus much harder to be in the world, because I felt like an outsider looking in at life. Although it took several years, I finally got the point where I adjusted to my "new normal" and began to feel like my old self. My interest in living fully returned, and I moved past the feeling that the other shoe was going to drop.

My Second Diagnosis

The years flew by, with me working, traveling, and making the most of each day. Overall, it was a great time. The downside was that by early 2010, I had lost both of my parents. Perhaps because my husband and I never had children of our own, I was always attached to my mom and dad. It took a long while for me to accept that they were gone.

In 2014, what ended up helping me recover from the loss I felt every day was my decision to write a book. It was to be a primer about the tenets of *A Course in Miracles* (*ACIM*), the spiritual tome I credit with helping me heal from my first bout with cancer in 2006. With an interest in all things "spiritual," I met a lot of people who were familiar with *ACIM*, but few seemed to really understand its core teachings. Because I had been studying it since 2003, I felt I had mastered it to the point where I was able to share what I had learned with other survivors. So, that summer, I sat down to write.

I was not sure how to begin and ended up with pages of narrative and no clear outline or structure. To say it was slow going is a bit of an understatement. About ten days after I settled into writing, I learned that a federal agency contract, on which I had been bid as the person to perform the work, had come through. The start date was immediate, and I was told to report to the Project Office the following week. As it turned out, the contract was a three-year deal, which is fairly atypical in the freelance world. I was excited about the prospect of having guaranteed income for such a long period of time and felt certain I would have no problem writing my book while holding down the full-time job.

As I got up to speed at work, I knew that writing my book would have to be put on the back burner. Those three years were exciting and extremely challenging. The agency in which I found myself was experiencing major disagreements between its management and union factions. Since our office was tasked with communicating to the entire staff, and there seemed to be little agreement on either side about how proposed changes would transpire, the atmosphere was never relaxed. While I tried to make the most of the opportunity and did enjoy the work, I cannot say I was unhappy when the contract came to an end. In early October 2017, with my "three-year tour" complete, I was back to freelancing. Although it felt good to have had the opportunity to be a communications specialist at a federal agency, I was worn out. The three years of stress took their toll; I was in need of a rest. I decided to postpone looking for paid work and started writing the book again.

Three weeks into my author staycation, I woke up with a terrible pain in my lower back. After several days of sitting on pillows, I went for a CT scan. When the technician came back with a somber look on his face, I knew I had a real problem. The next day, the doctor called to tell me that I had a tumor in my L5 vertebra and that it was probably cancer. Several weeks later, I was back at the Lombardy Cancer Center at Georgetown Hospital, where the tests confirmed that the tumor was metastatic breast cancer in my spine.

It took several months to get through all of the testing and a few months more to complete the targeted radiation and undergo the procedure to rebuild my vertebra, but I was determined to get beyond the disease. I was not sure how I would do that, so knowing that another full-time job was probably out of the question, I took time off to come to terms with my "new normal." Eventually, I decided to dedicate myself to finishing my book. After an almost two-year hiatus, I sat down at my kitchen table to write in September 2019.

The day before Thanksgiving, I turned in my first draft of *Put Cancer Behind You*. During the two months I spent writing, I was still having blood tests every couple of weeks. What I noticed in each report was that the cancer level in my blood was diminishing with each test. When I went to see my oncologist in February 2020, she told me that I was in remission. I was elated. While I never expected to die from the disease, I did not expect to get well by immersing myself in the teachings of *ACIM* either. I was more than a little curious to find out exactly how the miraculous turnaround occurred and how I could maintain my good health going forward. With a little digging, what became clear to me is that my health transformation involved "energetic frequency."

The Energetic Flow of Good Health

When I was writing *Put Cancer Behind You*, I spent several hours a day writing and several more researching each chapter to ensure that the information I included was correct and congruent with *ACIM*. That is how I went into remission: sitting at my kitchen table, typing on my computer. It did not involve meditation, eating or drinking anything different or "special," or doing any kind of exercise. Quite the opposite – I was a complete couch potato during the writing period because I was working quickly to meet my editor's deadlines. I also never went to a healing session or took any new drug.

When I tell people this, many have a difficult time accepting it, because we are taught that healing comes from outside of ourselves. But my remission from a terminal illness – as well as the disappearance of all the fear that I had as a cancer patient who did not know how long her life would be – is proof that all healing comes from within. It was wonderful to know that I did not have to die from cancer, but I also knew that to remain cancer free, I had to understand what happened to me so that I could keep doing whatever helped me get well.

This led to my next big question: "How *do* I stay healthy?" It is one thing to be cured but another to remain that way. With what I knew about stress and how it impacted my life, I understood that to remain in good health, I needed to understand exactly how I healed. I never wanted to experience cancer again and it was that desire which prompted me to start my research.

If you are willing to entertain the idea that every fear can be banished and every disease cured, it is natural for you to ask the question, "How?" What I learned is that the answer comes by changing a few key things in your life. It may take a little bit of time, but if you put your mind to it, I guarantee that it will be the best investment of your time that you have ever made. Why? Because once you have been sick, you understand that a life lived in fear of disease or with disease is no life at all.

If you are interested in learning how I put terminal cancer behind me and am now living above the fear of any disease, and you want to be able to do the same, then consider this book my gift to you.

CHAPTER 3

THE PROCESS OF MOVING FROM FEAR TO FEARLESSNESS

Regardless of what anyone tells you, you can live a joyful, disease-free life. When I put myself into remission from terminal cancer, I quickly realized the magnitude of what happened. I also felt that if I could do it, anyone could cure themselves of any disease. They just needed to know how. My first book, *Put Cancer Behind You*, is a spiritual guide to true healing. But I also know that my brand of spirituality as a student of *A Course in Miracles* is not everyone's cup of tea. For that reason, I am sharing what I learned *and* giving you the some of the science behind the spirituality. It all comes down to energy and knowing how to use it.

Energy is life. Your understanding of how it connects everything is what will put you in the driver's seat when it comes to creating good health. When you expand your understanding of your mind and body and learn how they are connected to the world and all that exists beyond, you will be able to make choices that support the life you want. This information is the key to real personal power. It will enable you to stop guessing about how to be healthy and put you on track to directing the flow of your life with conscious intent. You have the power to create the life you want and achieve the outcome you desire. I designed this book to teach you how to do just that, so you never fear disease again.

In the next chapter, I begin with a discussion about the nature of energy, which includes information about energetic vibration and frequency. It is also where I present the frequency range for a healthy human body and list the frequencies of certain diseases.

In Chapter 5, we take a look at what impacts your ability to achieve and maintain a healthy frequency. This includes what you eat and drink.

Once you understand the true nature of your mind and how your frequency impacts both the world and the universe, you can make choices that lead to unstoppable good health. Chapter 6 is where we cover this information.

In Chapter 7, I discuss how your beliefs, thoughts, and emotions impact your frequency and, therefore, your health. It is also where I introduce the process of identifying negative beliefs in order to acknowledge them and then replace them with healthier thoughts.

Chapter 8 is all about recognizing your power, with the understanding that you are responsible for everything which shows up in your life. It is in this chapter that we also define true forgiveness and look at the role it plays in helping you to get healthy and stay healthy.

In Chapter 9, we cover how you create your world. I also provide tips on how to protect yourself from unhealthy hazards in your environment and create a high frequency lifestyle.

Chapter 10 provides more tips on self-care so that you can lead a life above the battlefield of disease. In this chapter, I also share my routine for staying disease free.

I want to stress that good health is a choice we each make moment by moment, day by day. When you master your mind, you master your body – not the other way around. Mind is the level of cause, and body is the level of effect. The energetic frequencies of both your mind and body determine the health you experience throughout life. If you want to start your journey to self-mastery and stop being afraid of disease, and if you are ready to lean in to living a healthy life going forward, regardless of anything that happens in the world around you or the genes you carry, then get ready to focus on creating the life you want.

CHAPTER 4

ENERGY AND HUMAN
FREQUENCY FUNDAMENTALS

In our search for answers about life on Earth and across the universe, scientists have examined, accepted and rejected a multitude of theories about the nature of reality, gravity and energy. Thanks to Einstein's equation, $E = mc^2$, which equates energy with matter, we understand that everything in existence is energetic. While many unanswered questions about the nature of reality remain, the scientific community now believes that the universe is made up of energetic subatomic particles and waves that are constantly in motion at certain speeds, which is to say, everything that exists vibrates at a specific "frequency."

Frequency is measured in hertz (Hz). One hertz is one revolution or cycle per second. One megahertz (MHz) is one million cycles per second and a gigahertz (GHz) is one billion cycles per second. Whatever moves quickly is of a high frequency, and whatever moves slowly is of a lower frequency. The denser an object is, the more slowly it vibrates. The lighter something is, the faster its vibration. It is frequency that allows energy to express itself in any form, from particles and atoms to biological life, planets, and galaxies. Inventor and physicist Nikola Tesla underscored the importance of this with his comment, "If you want to find the secrets of the universe, think in terms of energy, frequency, and vibration."

The Nature of Energy

What exactly is energy? It is difficult to define in a way that is easily understood because energy is not a thing. It is an attribute or trait of both solid matter, such as physical bodies, and nonmatter, such as thoughts and emotions. The only form of energy that can be seen with our eyes is white light, but all energy can be observed and measured indirectly through its effects on whatever acquires, loses, or possesses it.

Energy falls into two categories: kinetic and potential. Kinetic energy is the energy something has because it is in motion – for example, a windmill or a car driving down the road. Potential energy is that which is stored in an object due to its position, like a ball you hold in your hand. When you let the ball drop, the potential energy converts to kinetic energy. According to the first law of thermodynamics, energy cannot be created or destroyed. However, it can and does change from one form to another. This can be demonstrated by a cyclist who pedals up one side of a hill and coasts back down the other. In doing this, the cyclist's kinetic energy of peddling changes into potential energy at the top of the hill and is available as kinetic energy for when the cyclist begins to peddle again.

The Frequency of the Human Body

When it comes to the human body, every atom, molecule, cell, and tissue is energetic; every thought and emotion is as well. When these are superimposed on each other, they create the human body energy field. Some people know it as our "aura" and others call it our "energy vortex." This electromagnetic field plays

Maria B. Barnes

an important role in your health because the field is profoundly affected by all the thoughts and emotions that emanate from your mind. It is these frequencies, which originate in the non-physical, that have the most significant effect on the frequency of your body. In short, what you think and feel are critical in determining whether you attract the frequency of good health or disease.

The first person to measure the frequency of the human body and its parts was Bruce Tainio, a microbiologist who developed a line of natural products to enhance the health of crops. Besides studying microbial activity in soil, Bruce was interested in quantum energy and, in his spare time, studied electromagnetic frequencies. In 1992, he built a machine called the BT3 Frequency Monitoring System, which he used to measure the bio-electrical frequencies of plant nutrients. Over time, he built several machines to measure various frequencies, including those associated with the human body.

As fate would have it, Bruce was an acquaintance of Gary Young, the founder of Young Living Essential Oils. In his book, *Aromatherapy: The Essential Beginning*, Gary writes that he was interested in finding out how different essential oils could be used to treat various illnesses and help clients reverse disease and unhealthy conditions. In the early 1990s, Gary learned that the bio-electrical frequencies of the oils could be measured in hertz (Hz), megahertz (MHz), and kilohertz (KHz). At the time, he was testing the frequency of oils, but was not receiving consistent results. He mentioned this to Bruce, who offered to help him by retesting them using the BT3. While working together to measure the frequency of oils, Gary tells us that all of the tests that they conducted were measured in hertz.

In addition to measuring the vibrational frequency of essential oils, Gary and Bruce went on to use the BT3 to determine the average frequency of a healthy human body and its parts, as well as the frequency of certain diseases. The results led them to the conclusion that if a person could maintain a body frequency that mirrored the range of a healthy immune system, and their body was well oxygenated, that person could remain free of disease. Following are the frequencies for a healthy human body as determined by Bruce Tainio and Gary Young:

Genius brain	80–82 Hz
Brain frequency	72–90 Hz
Normal brain	72 Hz
Human body	62–78 Hz
Human body from the neck up	72–78 Hz
Human body from the neck down	60–68 Hz
Thyroid and parathyroid glands	62–68 Hz
Thymus gland	65–68 Hz
Heart	67–70 Hz
Lungs	58–65 Hz
Liver	55–60 Hz
Pancreas	60–80 Hz
Spleen	60–78 Hz
Liver	55–60 Hz
Stomach	58–65 Hz
Colon	70–78 Hz

It is clear from Tainio and Young's work that every part of a human body has an energy signature. So, what determines the vibrational frequency rate of your body's energy field? Both internal and external factors. While the air we breathe, the environment we live in, the food we eat, and the lifestyle that we lead all impact our health, it is our beliefs, thoughts, and emotions that have the greatest impact on our frequency and, therefore, our immune system.

As Tainio and Young discovered, the human body with a

healthy immune system vibrates within the frequency range of 62–78 Hz. At this frequency, the body is immune to any disease. Tainio and Young's measurements also demonstrated that bacteria, viruses, and disease of any kind exist only at frequencies below 60 Hz. That means they vibrate more slowly than healthy tissue, so their frequency is incompatible with a higher frequency. They simply cannot survive in the microbiomes of your body when you are vibrating at a higher frequency than their naturally lower frequency. It is only when the body's frequency dips below 60 Hz – due to an electromagnetic imbalance that alters specific vibrational frequencies of molecules and cells – that the immune system becomes compromised, and the frequency of the person becomes a match to the frequency of an illness.

According to Tainio and Young's research, the frequencies of certain diseases, conditions and the onset of death are as follows:

Colds and flu begin	57–60 Hz
Disease begins	58 Hz
Candida overgrowth begins	55 Hz
Epstein-Barr appears	52 Hz
Cancer begins	42 Hz
Death begins	20–25 Hz

Electromagnetic Imbalance in Your Body

How do our beliefs and thoughts create the electromagnetic imbalances in the body that lead to illness? It is important to understand that everything you think impacts your entire energy field. Negative thoughts and emotions about the people, places, and events in your life vibrate more slowly than loving thoughts. Over time, as you continue to make judgments, you are increasing the negative thoughts that are stored in your subconscious. Eventually, if the level of negativity outweighs the positive frequencies, your entire vibrational rate slows, which means that the frequency of your immune system becomes lower. That is when your immune system is open to being compromised.

Once your immune system is off, all the body's systems can be negatively impacted. For many people, the daily stress of our modern life is not conducive to maintaining a healthy immune system. The good news is that once you understand energy frequency and know how to raise yours, you are in in control of the frequency you emit.

Now that you have a basic understanding of energy and know the frequency range of good health, you can apply the information to yourself and lead the life you deserve. To prevent and/or cure any disease requires that you think high frequency thoughts. To support your high vibration thoughts, eat high-frequency foods and maintain a high-frequency lifestyle. This is not mysticism or magic. It is basic science combined with an understanding of your own power that can help you move forward and live a fearless life. The choice to use that power is in your hands.

CHAPTER 5

FEEDING A HIGH-FREQUENCY BODY

f you find yourself constantly worried about getting sick —
whether from a cold, the flu, or something as serious as cancer —
now is the time to turn that fear around. It starts by committing
to living a high-frequency life. Just as everything we think affects
our health, everything in our environment does too. By taking
control of what you think, eat, and drink, you can control your
frequency and, therefore, your health.

Food Matters

Proper nutrition is essential for a healthy body and everything we
eat plays a part in creating our frequency. So, what should you
eat to help keep your immune system healthy and your frequency
high? Ideally, food products that are organic. According to the
United States Department of Agriculture (USDA), which certifies
that organic foods are grown and processed according to federal
guidelines, produce may only be labeled organic if it is certified to
"have grown on soil that had no prohibited substances applied for
three years prior to harvest." This means it must have been grown
without the use of synthetic fertilizers and pesticides.

In 2014, the *British Journal of Nutrition* published a paper that evaluated 343 studies on the nutritive value of organic and nonorganic food. It concluded that organic foods are healthier because they contain up to 69 percent more antioxidants than nonorganic foods. This is significant as antioxidants have been found to help prevent heart disease, neurodegenerative disease, and cancer. Today, most people understand that fresh raw fruits, vegetables, nuts, and seeds contain a wide variety of vitamins, minerals, enzymes, and phytonutrients that our bodies need to function properly. But to maximize their nutritional benefits, you need to eat them as soon after harvest as possible, before their vitamin, enzyme, and antioxidant values deteriorate.

In 2008, when Walmart decided to begin buying more locally sourced produce, the firm issued a press release stating that an average meal travels 1,500 miles "before it gets to you." This led to numerous reports about how far produce travels, on average, from farm to table in the United States. The fact is that with so much produce sourced from a multitude of countries, due to growing seasons in different hemispheres, the actual number of miles that it travels to get to your plate could be much higher, depending on whether the product is coming from Central America, South America, Europe, Africa, or Asia.

According to an article that appeared in the *Chicago Times* on February 2, 2021, most produce loses 30 percent of its nutritional value within three days of harvest. This is important to know if you buy your produce at the local grocery store. Why? Because regardless of whether the produce you buy was grown organically, or through the use of conventional farming practices, the transportation time of the produce to the store is generally much longer than the time it takes for local farmers' markets or food co-ops to acquire their produce. The lesson here is to buy local whenever you can. It will probably be significantly more nutritious.

When it comes to animal products, what does "organic"

mean? USDA regulations for organic animal food products require the animals to have been raised in living conditions that accommodated their natural behaviors (like grazing in a pasture and not a feed lot). The animals must also have been fed 100 percent organic "feed and forage" and cannot have been given either antibiotics or hormones.

When I was being treated for cancer the first time, I worked with a nutritionist to ensure I was eating for good health and avoiding foods that could be detrimental to my healing. She explained to me that for food products to be considered organic, they must be free of artificial food additives like sweeteners, preservatives, artificial colors, and monosodium glutamate (MSG). She also let me know that organic milk and dairy products contain lower levels of saturated fats and slightly higher amounts of iron. They are also associated with a higher level of omega-3 fatty acids, which have been associated with the reduced risk of heart disease.

What else did the nutritionist tell me? Avoid eating processed sugar. If you do want to sweeten your food and beverages, use honey or maple sugar in moderation. Read the labels on the food you buy to look at the sugar content. You should also be on the lookout for anything that includes high-fructose corn syrup (HFCS), which is a type of fructose that comes from sugar cane. Why is HFCS bad for you? You will never see this in any literature from a food company, but it is metabolized differently than regular fructose from fruit and is a leading contributor to increased liver fat. According to the National Institutes of Health (NIH), "fatty liver disease can lead to liver inflammation and liver damage, resulting in a more aggressive disease called non-alcoholic steatohepatitis (NASH). NASH can progress to scarring of the liver (cirrhosis), as well as liver cancer and liver failure."

My work with the nutritionist prompted me to continue researching the food choices I was making. What became clear is that 75 percent of your diet should include organic, non-genetically modified (non-GMO) fruits and vegetables that are locally sourced and freshly harvested. Fruits and vegetables that have a high-water content are preferable. You should also include foods that are dense, such as legumes, nuts, whole grains, and seeds.

Over the years, this led to my learning about the energetics of plant and animal food products. When it comes to the energetics of the meat, poultry, and fish we consume, the energy frequency of the animal's life continues with the carcass. That means that if the animal lived a healthy life and ate grass out on a range or swam freely in the ocean, its body mass vibrated at a higher frequency during its lifetime than a cow or salmon that spent its life in a feed lot or a contained pool.

The bottom line is that the healthiest choice for a steak or other animal product comes from one that was raised organically. And just as the nutritional value of produce diminishes over time, it is also best to buy from a butcher who sources the products from local farms, which helps guarantee less time from farm to table. The same goes for chickens, pigs, hogs, turkeys, or any other animal raised in cramped, unhealthy conditions. Free-range meat is the way to go. Fish should be wild-caught and sustainable.

Because Bruce Tainio's career was focused primarily on producing healthy plants, he and Gary measured the frequency of certain plant foods. The result of their measurements showed the following:

Fresh fruits/vegetables	20–27 Hz
Fresh herbs	20–27 Hz
Dried foods	15–22 Hz
Dried herbs	15–22 Hz
Processed/canned food	0 Hz

They noted that fresh foods and herbs can have frequency as high as 80 Hz if grown organically and eaten within several hours of being harvested. I want to add that cooking fruits and vegetables above 118 degrees Fahrenheit has been shown to lower their frequency. If boiled, their frequency is lowered significantly. If they are steamed, they retain a somewhat higher frequency.

Higher-frequency foods include:

- Organic fruits and vegetables
- Raw herbs
- Sprouts
- Wild berries
- Raw cacao (no sugar added)
- Maple syrup
- Mushrooms
- Probiotics (naturally fermented sauerkraut, pickles, kombucha)
- Soaked and sprouted raw nuts, seeds, and legumes
- Cold pressed organic oils (coconut, flax, avocado, sesame, olive)

Lower-frequency foods include:

- Genetically modified (GMO) food
- White rice and flours
- Sugars and artificial sweeteners
- Processed, packaged, and/or canned food
- Vegetable oils
- Frozen food
- Pasteurized cow milk, yogurt, and cheese
- Deep-fried food
- Microwaved food

Beverages Matter

What you drink also matters. Start your day with a glass of filtered water and try to drink at least eight glasses of filtered water every day. Organic herbal teas (preferably green) and freshly squeezed juices are also high-frequency beverages. I often add lemon slices to my water, which is also great for detoxifying the liver.

If you are looking for a beverage that is high in antioxidants and immune-supportive, consider matcha, a Japanese green tea powder. It has a slightly bitter taste and a vibrant green color that comes from the leaves' high chlorophyll levels. Gram for gram, matcha is considered one of the most powerful antioxidants in nature.

Dairy should only be consumed if the cow is 100 percent grass fed. Choose organic, non-GMO, and unsweetened plant-based milks whenever possible. Alternatives include oat, hazelnut, cashew, macadamia, almond, coconut, rice, and hemp milks.

Drinking coffee and alcohol lowers your frequency, as does consuming sugar. If you want to achieve or maintain a high frequency, limit your consumption of both. Drink unsweetened herbal/green tea. If you like plant-based milks, choose those that are not artificially sweetened.

Higher-Frequency Beverages

- Fresh-pressed green vegetable juice
- Fresh-pressed fruit juice (no sugar added)
- Filtered water
- Unsweetened plant-based drinks

Lower-Frequency Beverages

- Caffeinated drinks
- Coffee
- Soft drinks

- Alcohol
- Sweetened drinks
- Pasteurized milk

When shopping for food, choose as wisely as you can and then cook and eat with love. Before sitting down to a meal, take a moment to offer your deep appreciation and give thanks for what is before you. If the food is not organic, this will draw light into it. Why? Because food that is raised through large commercial agriculture practices has a lower vibration. Your gratitude and prayer can help restore a higher vibration to it, which benefits you once you have consumed it.

CHAPTER 6

THE TRUTH ABOUT YOU
AND EVERYTHING ELSE

When was the last time you felt completely well? By that I mean, when was the last full day you did not experience some form of fear or anxiety? How long ago was it that you spent a day without anger, pain, or fear of any kind? When was the last time you felt truly at peace? When was the last time you did not need a doctor of any kind? If you want to be truly healthy, you must learn to put fear, in all of its many forms, behind you. To do that, you will need to unlearn a lot of what you learned and took to heart. Without fear, you will be living at a frequency that is higher than any you have experienced for quite some time.

Your True Frequency versus
Your Current Frequency

The first belief that you may never have been taught but need to accept going forward is that you are an eternal, energetic being. Your true nature is spirit, and you will always exist. The frequency you hold for all eternity is that of pure love. So, what is the frequency of love? That of God, which is the highest frequency there is. Since God, or Source, is All That Is, everything it creates is made by love, from love, for love.

Unfortunately, as a being who is living in a physical body, you do not vibrate at the frequency of love on a constant basis. Why? Because of what you believe. Beliefs, thoughts, and emotions all have their own frequency, which brings us to another belief you were never taught: all disease begins and ends in the mind. This idea, that illness originates in our minds and is not something that happens to us randomly, is a revolutionary idea even in the 21st century. It is certain that few in the traditional Western medical community were taught to understand the role our minds play in our well-being. But despite what any doctor tells you, it is your beliefs, thoughts, and emotions that dictate what you attract and manifest.

Why is that true? Because the body in and of itself does nothing. It takes all of its direction from the brain. You do not bat an eyelash without a neurologic prompting from the brain, and brains are directed by the thoughts and beliefs in our minds. Everything that happens inside the body – from the beating of our hearts to all the other physiological functions that keep our bodies going – is managed at the unconscious level of the mind. So, to be clear, the body does not run the mind. The unconscious mind runs everything that happens to the physical body, including the creation and disappearance of disease.

The Nature of Our Mind

To understand how this works, let's take a brief look at the nature of our minds. The mind is divided into two parts: the conscious and unconscious mind. Our conscious mind represents roughly 5 to 10 percent of our thoughts, while the unconscious part represents the other 90 to 95 percent. It is there, in the unconscious part of our minds, that all of the information we absorb becomes our internal representations.

Maria B. Barnes

According to a study undertaken by researchers at the Brain and Mind Institute at the University of Western Ontario in Canada, humans receive around eleven million bits of information per second. It is way too much to acknowledge consciously, so all of it gets processed in our subconscious mind using our internal filters. This is how we delete, distort, and generalize everything into beliefs that match what we are programmed to accept by society. These beliefs generate thoughts, which then generate emotions and action.

Because we each have slightly different internal filters, our perceptions of something will often vary. This explains why we can see the same situation differently from the person standing next to us. We both process the incoming information through our unique filters. Due to the different beliefs in our subconscious mind that contribute to our own personal viewpoints, we come up with different models of the world.

Your model of the world includes all of your stored internal representations: the beliefs, thoughts, and memories that are made up of pictures, sounds, feelings, tastes, and smells. These are the basis for the mind–body connection. We use them constantly as a reference for interpreting everything that shows up in our daily life.

How many thoughts do we have on any given day? According to a study funded by the National Science Foundation, an average person has between 12,000 and 60,000 thoughts a day. What kinds of thoughts are these? The study determined that up to 80 percent of our thoughts are negative and 95 percent of those are repetitive. With such a high percentage of the thoughts running rampant in our unconscious mind being negatively repetitive, the next question has to be, "How is this impacting my health?" The answer is greatly. If enough of your thoughts are positive and high frequency, your body remains healthy. But when your thoughts are primarily negative, this causes your body's frequency to dip.

Cause and Effect

To be powerfully creative, you need to understand cause and effect. Cause is the level of the mind. It is from here that energy becomes materialized into the world. If you want to cure a disease, which is some form of fear made manifest from the level of cause, you must root out the repetitive beliefs and emotions that brought it into existence. Until you do, the disease can come back. This is why there can be a recurrence of every lower-frequency health condition, from colds to cancer.

To change how we think about our health and understand our ability to stay healthy will take time. Why? Because as we grew up, none of us ever learned that we create our world. In fact, quite the opposite. However, it is the sum of all your thoughts, along with everyone else's, that creates the world. This means that the world is the level of effect. In short, whatever shows up in the world only does so after trillions of repeated thoughts and their associated emotions become energetically dense enough, or slow down, to manifest as something physical.

Understanding this certainly gives me a deeper appreciation for why things happen, especially in different parts of the world. What each of us thinks and feels is important, and what we think and feel as a collective is critical. Just imagine what would happen if we were all to start believing more loving thoughts about ourselves and each other. Hopefully, we will live to see that in our lifetime, as the collective consciousness of "us" evolves.

Creation versus Miscreation

What does creation versus miscreation mean? It boils down to how you choose to use time. Creation is always love-focused, while miscreation is always fear-focused. Creation comes from high-frequency thoughts that are positive, while miscreation is low frequency and negative.

When you understand that how you choose to focus your

Maria B. Barnes

thinking impacts what shows up in your life, you become mindful of what you are thinking. Judgment is negative. It always takes you away from love and toward separation from Source. So, the real work we have before us is to monitor our thoughts and keep them positive. Although you are contributing energy to the entire collective all the time, what appears in your own "slice of life" is what is resonating from beliefs that are near and dear to your heart.

It is also impossible to upgrade your frequency and prevent or dismiss disease if you are always talking about it or thinking about it. That is another way we all miscreate with our minds. But once you start to turn long-standing negativity into neutrality, new doors will open for you. This is possible when you accept what shows up in your life instead of judging it.

The Law of Attraction

It is important to understand that from an energy standpoint, your body is an antenna. It literally receives and emits energy constantly. What is being communicated? The energy frequency of you, which is made up of your beliefs, thoughts, and emotions as well as the energy of all your body's physical tissue. Yes – each and every second of the day – the electromagnetic vibrational frequencies you hold are being broadcast out across the universe. More importantly, whatever frequency you emit is what will be returned; in short, it will be a frequency match. This is known as the universal law of attraction, or "like attracts like."

Another way to describe the law of attraction is as the energetic potential gathering and delivery system for your physical experience. It is always responding to your vibrational offering and everything that happens around and to you is due to the vibration that you are emitting. Your frequency is literally your way of choosing what you will experience next.

What about all your unfulfilled desires? How do you get more of what you want in life? The question you need to ask yourself is whether your desires are resonating at a frequency that is greater than you allow yourself to accept, even though some part of you wants to resonate with it. For example: you dream of winning the lottery, but never have. Why not? Because it is not a vibrational match. If this happens frequently, if you are mentally asking for something to come your way and it does not, to turn that around, you must focus on matching your frequency with the frequency of what you desire. As Albert Einstein put it, "Everything is energy and that's all there is to it. Match the frequency of the reality you want, and you cannot help but get that reality. It can be no other way. This is not philosophy. This is physics." Indeed, it is.

The Holographic Universe

The law of attraction means the universe is holographic, a mirror of the collective mind. Since the holographic universe responds instant by instant to the frequency of what you and everyone else broadcast, it sends back whatever matches the frequency of the collective, in general, and your frequency, in particular. That is why giving is the same as receiving. On a daily basis, whatever you broadcast to everyone and everything will come back to you in the form of people, places and events that match your frequency. The universe always gives you what you feel worthy to receive.

Go back to the feeling of being in love. Don't you feel great just remembering that feeling? Take your time and feel into it. Revel in the boundless exhilaration of being in love! It is a wonderful emotional place to be. When you are fully there, doesn't everything else seem much less important and bothersome? How can it be other than high vibe living when love takes over your world? Suddenly, you find that something you were wanting to have in your world, before you fell in love, shows up. Why? Because it was still in your vortex. It was manifested at a different frequency, out in the field of pure potentiality. When you raised your vibration by opening your heart, it became a match. In essence, you allowed yourself to have it in this reality.

That is how the universe works. You have a desire, the universe responds, but it cannot become manifest until the frequency of what you want matches up with the frequency you are holding. So, pay attention to what is in your world. If you do not like what is showing up, you need to change your beliefs, thoughts, and emotions to project a different frequency in order to attract different experiences, and then allow them to manifest by holding the high vibration.

The truth is, because we live in a resonating universe where everything is connected, we must be conscious about everything we think, say, and do. Like everything else you want, having good health requires maintaining a healthy vibrational frequency by selectively sifting through your thoughts so that you focus on tuning into your highest desired vibrational experience.

This is also what makes it possible to stop being fearful of disease. When you consciously stop focusing on being scared of getting sick and keep focusing on the good health that you want to experience, you can turn around the low frequency of fear. The power of your positive thoughts is what raises your body's frequency and literally puts you above the battleground of disease.

The Beginning of Disease

If you concentrate on sending out positive thoughts and the change you are hoping for does not occur, it is because the energy in your field is blocked. You are not in a state of "allowing" so that what you asked for can manifest. Disease begins when the thoughts behind the blockage are not put back into balance. If the flow is not restored, poor health develops. It takes a long time for disease to begin. In fact, it takes years for a disease like cancer to develop to the point of doing harm.

When I sat down with the oncologist to discuss my cancer, he told me that I probably had the cancer for eight to ten years before it was discovered. I had a difficult time accepting that news. It made me question my entire life and the decisions I was making. In my case, I did not manifest cancer because I was worried about getting sick. It was the years of stress and constant worry about everything else in my life that took down my frequency and negatively impacted my immune system. I now agree with what research tells us: it takes up to ten years for cancer to go from one cell to a detectable lesion. I now admit that my life was stress-filled for a good decade before my cancer became evident.

The good thing about knowing how long it takes for a disease like cancer to develop is that if you are committed to reversing the negativity in your body's energy field during that time, you will be able to reverse the condition, and the disease will never manifest for you.

Another critical point is that since you have the power to manifest disease, you also have the power to cure it. This is how I became healthy after I was told I had terminal cancer: I literally thought myself well. I did not set out to do that, but it happened because the thoughts I was thinking were high frequency as I was writing my book, and I maintained that frequency for several months. As Einstein said, the frequency I broadcasted came back to me. It is simple physics. The consistency of the vibration over a certain period of time unblocked the negative energy flow and rebalanced my field. When you believe you can do this, you will also be able to raise or lower your vibrational frequency at will.

Why the Present Matters

Understand that whatever thought you focus your mind on is what you get more of. This is literally how you create your life. Because of that, it is critical to be fully aware of what you are thinking each and every moment. Pay attention to the thoughts that cross your mind. When a negative thought surfaces, if you do not ignore it immediately, you are giving energy to it. This means that any belief or emotion associated with that thought becomes increased in its strength.

Since you create the future by what is in your mind at the present moment, whatever you are focusing on right now is what you are energetically extending into your future. This is a critical point when it comes to creating good health, but few understand that. It is why a poor health condition can become chronic rather than cured. It happens because the person is extending unconscious negative beliefs and thoughts about their health moment by moment rather than using their time to think about good health with conscious intent. I do not believe anyone consciously sets out to create poor health. But because of unconscious miscreation, many do it on a regular basis. For that reason, it is important to understand how you miscreate, so you can prevent fearful thoughts in your unconscious from driving the boat.

You may not realize this, but every thought you have ever had, every memory, is stored somewhere in your subconscious mind. These show up and play out every day as strategies our minds use to navigate life. They are what create and sustain our model of the world. If you are being fearless and loving, you will attract more of that and enjoy a positive model of the world. If you do not replace thoughts that do not serve you, you can guarantee that they will be of disservice to you in the future. So, be mindful, be fully present, and be aware of what you are thinking moment by moment. Focus on the positive, on thoughts that make you feel good, eager about life and excited for your future. The point of power is only ever in the present. Use your present wisely, in order to move into a healthy, happy future.

Unstoppable Good Health

I want to emphasize that we were all taught to buy into the idea that what occurs in our lives is merely the luck of the draw and is separate from us. We were sold a bill of goods because nothing could be further from the truth. It is time to quit believing you have no power and are at the mercy of whatever is "out there" in the world. Your life *is* your creation.

How do you counteract devastating disease and all the fears you have about getting sick or your inability to be well? By being unrelenting in making the choice for love. Instead of looking outside of yourself for love, look at yourself. See yourself as worthy of love. Take a few minutes and feel into it. Allow yourself to be the object of your desire. Talk to your cells and thank them for everything they do to keep you healthy. They are always listening. They understand the frequency of every thought you have, so mentally tell them, "I love you." Make it a point to send them love every day. See that positive white light energy pulsing through each and every cell of your body. Feel your love for them and watch them respond to you. Keep feeling how miraculous every cell in your body is, how wonderful they all are as part of you. Just "think love." Practice this by appreciating and honoring your body every day for several minutes. Visualize your healthy, vibrant self and shower it with all the high vibration you can muster. Every cell is so very deserving of this attention. This is how to heal and stay healed.

When you are upset by anything, take the time to step back and look at what you are thinking, what you are feeling, and what your beliefs are. Take stock of what you need to stop believing so you can replace unloving thoughts with love. If you are constantly worried about your safety or someone else's, you need to sit down and address what you believe will occur. What is your fearful belief? Then ask yourself what the opposite and loving thought to it would be. Begin to make those thoughts your mantras for the day. Every time a fearful thought crosses your mind, catch it and replace it by repeating a loving one. Feel into the positive emotion it brings up. Make that your reality. When you do this, it does not take much time to stop being fearful and begin trusting that you and your loved ones are supported at every step on the journey through this world.

How do you counteract negative behaviors and words by others that bring down your frequency? Send them thoughts of peace and love. Why? Because their words and actions are a cry for love. They are your own cry for love and help in overcoming the negativity that you have not addressed. Since you need love and understand that to give is to receive, the only appropriate response to someone else's cry for love, no matter how it appears, is to give love. That will raise your frequency immediately.

To have a better future, bring your best self to every problem, person, situation, or event. Give all of your blessings and goodwill to whatever is in the moment. Be your highest self. The sword is only ever hanging over your own head.

Frequency Alignment

Begin to see everything that shows up for you in life as a gift that deserves your clearest, kindest response. If you are in alignment with your highest self, everything in your life will be "in the flow." It will be easy and effortless. This puts you in a state of grace. It is your "meant to be." If, however, you find yourself not being relaxed or fearless, you need to turn that around. Pay attention to how you feel and make a commitment to bring your best self to every instant. Fears are challenges you put on your own table so that you can address them. Why? Because challenges are merely opportunities presented once again. Where you made a lesser choice before, you can make a better choice now – and hopefully, the optimal choice.

Your thoughts and emotions are good indicators of your

vibrational frequency. If you are afraid of getting sick, or fear that disaster could strike, and do not feel up to the task of turning anything around, accept where you are emotionally. It's okay to not be okay. When you are ready, you can begin to work on turning your fear into positivity. In the book *Ask and It Is Given* by Esther and Jerry Hicks, the couple offer a scale by which to gauge your emotions. I use it whenever I need to upgrade mine. The scale goes from the low end of fear, grief, depression, despair, and powerlessness all the way up to the high end of joy, knowledge, empowerment, freedom, love, and appreciation. If you are in a state of depression, it is unlikely that you will be able to jump right into feeling joy, love, and appreciation. But by allowing yourself to feel what you are feeling and then working up the scale, emotion by emotion, you will eventually find yourself in a place where you are peaceful and upbeat.

When you choose to align with your soul purpose in life, you have the confidence to take control of where you are heading. You are in a position to make choices that are high frequency because you are thinking loving thoughts about yourself and everything out in the world. A mind aligned with love is the most creative force in the universe. That is your true frequency: love. So, understand and accept that you can bring a happy, healthy dream into being. Be mindful; be strong; and choose to be the wonderful, magnificent being that you really are.

Exercise: Gratitude-filled day

The law of attraction never sleeps; therefore, with every thought you have in every moment, focus on creating good health and abundance. Do this by being grateful. When you are grateful, you are acknowledging that which you already possess.

It is a new day; one in which you are grateful for being healthy and excited about life. Begin to prioritize this day by thinking about what you want more of in your life. Be discerning. What is it that makes you feel good? What will uplift you and bring you joy? Focus on whatever that is by feeling into it: the joy, the happiness, the anticipation of your wonderful, new day. As you feel the high vibrations of this wellness, allow yourself to be more appreciative of everything and everyone in your world. Give thanks for all of your friends and family. Continue by extending thoughts of appreciation for your work, your opportunities for creativity and connection, and the fact that today *is one of the best days of your life*. This sets you up energetically to receive all that you desire.

Keep giving thanks as you move through your day, sending out thoughts of gratitude for your good health and your happy, abundant life. The holographic universe will keep returning to you that which matches the frequency of what you project. It is you reaping that which you have sown. So be mindful of how you are using your mind and think beautiful, inspired thoughts to bring you what you want more of: love.

CHAPTER 7

ADDRESSING YOUR FEARS

F ear is a state of consciousness that is incompatible with feeling happy, relaxed, and healthy. That is why whenever you feel anger, anxiety, worry, or irritation surfacing, you need to release it as quickly as possible. The more time you spend monitoring your unloving thoughts and consciously replacing them with loving affirmations, the quicker your fears will disappear, and your health will improve.

It takes courage and dedication to look within and address low frequency beliefs that create everything you do not want more of, especially disease. For many of us, this is a new endeavor, and we do not know how to do it. When I was diagnosed with cancer the second time, I knew I needed to understand where it came from if I was going to "kick it." I had an inkling of how powerful our minds are, but it had not sunk in deep.

The diagnosis made me take a hard look at how I was living my life and handling or not handling everything that showed up in my world. I started by writing down what was making me feel good and what was making me feel awful. It became clear that I was under a lot of stress. The notebook I used for these writings was my "Discovery Journal." Writing in this notebook is important and it is a tool I still use to maintain a high frequency. It is where I record the thoughts I have when I am triggered. I recommend that you start one, too.

Your Discovery Journal

The purpose of the Discovery Journal is to have a place where you can identify unhealthy beliefs and thoughts that are swirling around in your subconscious. Once you are aware of them, you can replace them with others that are healthy and positive. Doing this work will help you overcome the low frequency programs running in your mind so you can move beyond fear.

When it comes to creating and maintaining good health, it is important to look at your greatest fears. These are fairly easy to identify; just the thought of them puts you on edge. If you are fearful of getting sick and are stressed by being in a crowded space near other people, afraid that you will catch something from them, you need to take some time to sit down with your Discovery Journal. This is your opportunity to deconstruct your thoughts about your power to create and maintain good health. To master what happens to your body, you need to master your mind. Why? Each time that fear surfaces, you are projecting the unconscious belief that you are powerless to prevent getting sick out into the universe.

Use the journal to write down the thoughts that are surfacing in your mind about disease and death. Then, write down how each one made you feel when it came to mind. If you are being honest with yourself, you will see that you feel your salvation lies outside of you. This is you confirming a belief in your powerlessness to prevent yourself from getting sick without taking some form of medication or other precaution. In placing your ability to stay well outside of yourself, you are stating you have no faith in your own ability to create good health for yourself. You are stating you are not in control of your mind or your body, which opens you up to being a victim of the world around you.

That is a dangerous state of mind in which to exist. It is dangerous to your health because powerlessness is a low-frequency vibe that actually increases the odds of you getting sick. Now, this is not to say that if you break a bone or find yourself sick with a debilitating chronic disease that you do not seek medical attention – of course you do. But to get well and stay well, you will need to raise your vibration.

Keep telling yourself, "I am powerful and loving. I am in good health and I am not fearful of disease. I am living in a state of wellness." Repeat that thought every time your fear surfaces – about getting sick or about an illness you currently have. Remember to talk to your body's cells and send them love. If you keep it up, after a while, you will stop being afraid and start relaxing into your immune system's ability to get and stay healthy. You will raise your vibration above the frequency of fear and disease and reach the frequency of good health.

Uncover Your Beliefs

Whenever you find yourself reacting negatively to something someone says or does, step back and assess the situation. By giving yourself this time to digest the experience, you are taking a step toward neutrality rather than reinforcing negativity with more negativity. Later, when you sit down with your journal, ask yourself, "How did I do today?" Write down what happened that made you feel insecure or upset and open to getting sick. Feel into the emotions you felt. Then ask, "How is that feeling a problem? What is this bringing up for me?" Write down the answer. Then ask yourself again, "How is this a problem?" Note what it brings up for you. It could be a memory from when you were five. Frequently, root beliefs around guilt, fear, shame and anger lie deep in the past.

Keep repeating this process until it brings you to the point where that which surfaces is a negative belief, a negative idea you have about yourself. It could be that you believe you need to compete for everything and that nothing will be handed to you. Why is that a problem? If you need to compete for everything, it implies lack, or a belief in a world of lack. How is that a problem? It means you are competing with everyone for limited resources. But since everyone is connected and part of Source, you are essentially competing with Source. How is that a problem? Because of the guilt you have about competing with Source. Why is that a problem? Because God might punish you for that thought. Why is that a problem? Because you might deserve the punishment. Once you delve into the negative beliefs stored in your subconscious, it becomes clear many of them are untrue and even crazy. The sooner you root them out, the better.

It is these unhealthy beliefs that result in the unconscious strategies you use to navigate your world. They are always at play as you move through your day, impacting your relationships with family, friends, and coworkers. So, when you look at something out in the world and acknowledge it as something you do not want to experience more of, the first step is to use your present moment to accept that you contributed thousands of unhealthy, subconscious thoughts to the collective that brought the condition into existence. Ask yourself, "Where does this situation out in the world match me? What are my beliefs that are being mirrored back to me?"

If you are fearful of getting sick, or get sick a lot, follow back all the worry thoughts that crop up around that. You will discover that you have a belief in sickness. When you think about catching a cold or getting the flu, observe why that thought crossed your mind. What was the situation that made you think that?

It is important to write down your thoughts about any negative thought that surfaces during the day. Did you do or say something that was unloving just before you had that thought?

Did someone else? What brought up the fear for you? Did you find out about someone's sickness and feel vulnerable to becoming sick? It could be that nothing about illness surfaced until you heard a negative newscast about ill health or watched a movie in which people were sick and dying. Anything that is not loving can bring up low-frequency fears.

Once you answer those questions, look at what each is telling you. How do you know you are reading the information correctly? You will have your answer when you admit how each thought makes you feel. Your emotions will not lie. If you are fearful about getting sick, you will feel fear. Ask yourself why you feel that way. With each answer, go a bit deeper into your mind. Keep asking how each thought makes you feel until you get to the root of the problem.

As you write down negative thoughts that trigger you, you may notice a pattern in things that keep cropping up. This is a clue that you have a blind spot – a belief that you have been hiding from yourself. It will show up in various ways. For example, the belief "I'm not good enough" may present as disease, a low-paying job, or an unloving relationship. It could show up as negative judgments by others of you. At some point in your self-discovery work, you will see that your beliefs about yourself include being unworthy and undeserving of love. You will know you are there when the answer to your review of how a belief makes you feel begins with "un" – unhealthy, unloved, unworthy, undesirable, unable, or unprotected. Even if the answer turns out to be something like the word "weak," "powerless," "ashamed," or some other negative adjective, the answer will match the frequency of the negative thought.

Most people focus their thoughts by observing whatever is happening around them without realizing that it is coming from them. If it is positive, they feel good. If it is negative, then they may feel some form of fear: anger, discomfort, insecurity, lack of trust, etc. This negative, low vibe feeling you have is what you are projecting out into the universe. Turn these around by telling yourself that you are worthy, that you do deserve love. Reinforce this by taking time throughout the day to tell yourself that you are loved and that you were made by love, from love, and for love. If possible, stand in front of a mirror and say it out loud. Proclaim your worthiness to the universe and promise yourself that you have nothing to fear. You are here to love life and enjoy your experiences. The more you build up your confidence in yourself, the more you will move gracefully through all that life has to offer and be a blessing to the world.

As you replace old thoughts about catching a cold or getting the flu with positive thoughts about being healthy and excited about life, you will raise your frequency and get sick less often. Tell yourself frequently every day, "I'm in perfect health and I feel great! I'm healthy, whole and healed." At some point, you will stop getting sick altogether because your immune system will be completely healthy. At that frequency, your body is invulnerable to disease. The point is that when you start to see yourself as the healer you really are, you will heal. It takes practice to change your beliefs, but over time, that is how to get healthy and stay healthy.

Protection from Deadly Disease

If you are afraid of getting cancer or some other disease that can maim or kill you, or if you think you might be in the process of creating a negative health event like a stroke or heart attack, go through the same process. Catch the fearful thought as it moves through your mind. It could be anything from, "Wow, I had better get my colonoscopy soon!" to, "If Jim had a heart attack and we are the same age, what about me?!" We all have things in our lives that trigger the emotion of fear. When it comes to disease, you must work through the beliefs that could manifest as disease.

Every review of your fear-based thoughts is to find out why

you are resisting good health. Is someone in your family sick and you believe you will be next? Do you have a genetic marker that you think will lead to poor health? Ask yourself what belief you hold that insists you are not powerful enough to be healthy. Remember that all serious disease takes a long time to manifest. It shows up after you project fear for a long period of time. So, be open to learning what each negative belief, thought, or emotion is showing you and commit to reversing it while you still have time.

When you get to the point where you believe you are healthy, whole, and healed, and when you understand that like attracts like, you will be able to focus your thoughts so that you attract only good health. We all hide things in our subconscious that we do not want to deal with and, for the most part, are unaware of. But the universe will show you your own unease, which can turn into disease. So, be grateful when you see these low frequency beliefs and thoughts mirrored in the people and events around you. It is how your higher self lets you know it is time to get rid of them.

As you go down this path, you will find that doing your mind training also makes you happy. In fact, to stop doing the work would be too painful because you got to a point where whatever you were doing before was not working. You searched for a better way, and this process puts you firmly on that path.

With enough examination, it is likely you will find that you hold a lot of untrue, unhealthy ideas about yourself and your own self-worth. If you need to talk to someone about your lack of self-love in order to turn that around, make an appointment with someone you trust to help you explore your beliefs.

Radical Acceptance

As you begin to examine and change your thoughts, new patterns in your life will emerge. It is also likely you will realize that you make judgments all day long, and the majority of them are fear based. What does this mean? That these thoughts are unloving. The opposite of love is fear, so if a thought is not 100 percent loving, it is demonstrating a belief you have that is some form of fear. Since fear is not justified in any form, to redirect your life and create wellness, you must step back from judgment in a radical way. That means you cannot judge *at all*. This is known as radical acceptance, and it is what helps to undo low frequency "attack thoughts" by becoming neutral.

In being radically accepting, you are acknowledging your God-given free will is at play, along with everyone else's. It is literally the thoughts and beliefs of the entire "collective mind" that are being projected outward and are creating our world. Never forget that we are all loving, creative, joyous beings who came here to express ourselves. When you fall short and your life is not as joyful as you would like, it is because you bought into some form of fear. But that is part of being human. So, embrace problems knowing that you are looking at something within yourself that is neither at peace nor loving and needs your attention. This makes transforming your mind your life's real work.

Perception Is Projection

Why is it important to remain nonjudgmental and project high-frequency thoughts when it comes to our health? Because perception is projection. The Swiss psychiatrist Carl Jung first introduced this concept in the twentieth century. He said, "We tend to take our most unconscious material and project it on people and events around us." This means that everything "out there" is an energetic thought that is projected outward from your subconscious mind. In essence, we are all projecting the beliefs we do not want to deal with onto other people so that we can feel better. Since the universe is holographic, it sends back a frequency match to what we project. That is why whatever appears out there is a perfect match to who we are, not who anyone else is. As Jung stated, we only project what is inside of us, so others can never appear to us as anything other than what we project them to be. This also means that it is impossible to perceive something that we are not, because we only project ourselves.

When you look across the room at someone and have a positive thought, that is you being positive about yourself. When you look across the room and have a negative thought, that is you being negative about yourself. Everyone else is your reflection of you. Few of us realize this is what is happening when we judge others. Most believe that our world, with all its people and events, is being done *to* them, not *by* them.

Once you understand "perception is projection," it is easy to understand why radical acceptance is so important. In radically accepting everything that shows up for you, you are demonstrating that you know there is nothing out there to attack except yourself. Everything in the universe is connected energetically; everyone you encounter in the world is another aspect of you. It is why the Golden Rule of "do unto others as you would have done unto you" is so important. Simply put, the other is you. That is also why your judgments are so damaging to you: you are never judging anyone except yourself. It is that condemnation which can eventually lead to poor health.

The Significance of Your Free Will

Understand that your life is your free will made manifest. That places you in control of *everything*. With your free will, you write, produce, and direct your life instant by instant. It is your personal movie, and the premise is simple: you reap what you sow. The gift in this is that once you know what is going on, you can turn it around if it is not to your liking. If you do not want to experience more of what you see up on the movie screen of your life, you can think different thoughts so you can write a different script and project a different movie.

It will take time to replace unhealthy thoughts with thoughts of love, but you have the power to make that change. Start to adore yourself. Feel how wonderful, creative and joyful you really are. Start to envision freedom, abundance, and vitality for yourself. Feel into it. Do that often enough and you will never be willing to go back to living a life that is "less" when what you deserve is "more." Love every day and the opportunities you have to be the expression of who you really are: a high-frequency, eternal being who was made from love, by love and for love. Follow your North Star. To thine own self be true!

Exercise: Reframe Beliefs for New Opportunities

Sit comfortably at a table with your Discovery Journal, open to a blank page. Write down the following paragraph and then read it out loud:

As a creative, eternal spirit, I am here to experience a full life. I choose to be my highest self while living in my physical body. I am committed to creating a healthy life that is full of joy, happiness, and love. I am committed to being fearless and am willing to look at my fears so I can replace them with love. I am healthy, healed, and whole. I give thanks for my great health, my abundance, and my amazing life. Amen.

Search your mind for any doubts that contradict your power to have a healthy life. List them in the journal and then go into meditation. Envision yourself in a beautiful garden or at the edge of a calm sea. Next to you is a beautiful chest. The label on it reads "My Fears about Disease." Open it and place the fears that just came up for you inside of it. Then close it, lock it and bless it. Allow two angels to take possession of it. As they lift the chest off the ground, watch them disappear with it into nothingness. Raise your eyes and look at the beauty that surrounds you, feeling that you are in perfect alignment with all life. You are safe. You are loved. You are healthy. Feel the love in your heart. Breathe it in deeply through your nose and exhale it gently through your mouth. Do this until you are completely relaxed and at peace.

When you are ready, open your eyes. Write down how you feel now that you have released your fears. Read the opening paragraph out loud once more, adding at the very end, "I am now above the frequency of disease. Amen."

CHAPTER 8

RIGHT THINKING FOR HIGH-FREQUENCY HEALTH

I can almost guarantee that although you are a powerful creator, you were never told that when you were growing up. The chance of it happening as an adult who spends a great deal of the day in a stressful work environment is even slimmer. The world has long been run by people who are interested in keeping you small and more easily controlled. What society took decades to teach you is the negative programming that repeats over and over in your subconscious mind and prevents you from stepping onto the stage and into the light. The gist of it all is that over the course of your childhood, you were taught to be fearful. You accepted that belief because it made you feel safe. As an adult, you have never questioned that belief or any of the other untruths that were fed to you. The good news is that although you accepted unloving, limiting beliefs about yourself that are patently untrue, you can change that. It is time to acknowledge that those beliefs no longer serve you and move fearlessly forward.

The Point of Power Is Always in the Present

I explained that we all create the future we will experience with every thought we have and that in order to have a healthy future, you need to undo the negative and project the positive. But to change anything, you must do it in the present moment. Why? Because the present is quite literally the only point of power there is.

When you reminisce about the past or project a fantasy thought into the future, you are misusing your mind's powerful ability to create and are negatively impacting the present. You are allowing your mind to operate on autopilot, unconsciously, instead of directing your path consciously through life. A happy memory is a present joy, but a sad memory is painful. Your subconscious mind will always control your thoughts and actions unless you reprogram it by uncovering thoughts which no longer serve you and then replacing them with healthier thoughts. This is accomplished by being fully present in each "now moment," which is every second of every day.

When you are present-focused, you are using time the way it is meant to be used: creating your future with positive intent. If you decide that you do not like what is showing up in some area of your life, stop living in the past. Understand that every time you go back to reimagine an unpleasant event, you are re-inflicting that pain on yourself. Your choice to use your present moment of power to regurgitate any hurtful memory will plant the seeds for that same frequency showing up in the future, and that can be extremely unhealthy. Likewise, every time you imagine some fearful future, you are setting the stage for its arrival.

To own your creative power and make full use of it, practice using the present moment to focus on what is right in your world instead of what is wrong. Concentrate on thinking about what you want to consciously materialize in your world. How do you start? By becoming aware of what you are feeling right now. Acknowledge your emotions by stating, "I feel _____ right now." Once you have established how you feel, shift your focus to how you want to feel, which should be more positive. Envision yourself in a more positive situation and feeling better. Concentrate on this for at least 17 seconds. Feel deeply into the more positive emotion. See yourself interreacting with others as you feel that better emotion. Tell yourself, "Now I feel _____."

Take your time as you feel into the positive emotion. The longer you spend doing the exercise, the faster the more positive thought can take hold. At the two-minute mark, the replacement thought becomes a belief. It is at this point that the amount of energy you are emitting is sufficient to create a new timeline in which that emotion can become your reality. If you stay in vibrational alignment with the positive thought and emotion, and practice feeling into it over the course of a week, you will be shifting seamlessly to a higher frequency timeline.

Whenever you feel that you do not have the health you want, find reasons to feel good. Look at the stories you are telling yourself, so you understand why you are choosing resistance. Remember: the majority of your thoughts are negatively repetitive. If you are like most people, you have been using them to navigate your world for decades. The result has led to patterns in relationships and behaviors that no longer serve you. Use your Discovery Journal to identify these negative thoughts so you can allow new experiences to unfold. Identify fears you know are holding you back and write down positive responses. To enhance the positive beliefs, read them out loud. End by singing your new beliefs at the top of your voice. Doing this exercise has the same effect as saying positive mantras out loud with gusto. When I am focusing on staying cancer free, you can bet that I work up from a happy statement to a joyous shout out about my own good health. When I do that, I know my own good health is unstoppable.

A New Vibrational Point of Attraction

Every day is a new vibrational point of attraction, a reset of the energy frequency your body emits and receives. To ensure it is positive, before you even get out of bed, tell yourself what a wonderful day you are going to have. State emphatically over and over how abundant, loving, kind, amazing, healthy, happy, and creative you are on this new day. Express how appreciative you are to have this day ahead of you. Acknowledge this day as being one of the best days you will ever have. You know you are blessed and will meet extraordinary people who are loving, kind, and honest. You will feel love throughout your day. It will be full of positive experiences. If anything negative does show up, you will use it to remind yourself of the good vibes you are creating. Keep coming up with reasons for why today is going to be one of the healthiest days of your life. Then go live it.

What about Judgment?

It is worth exploring judgment a bit further because it is so detrimental to your psyche and overall health. When you judge anything, several things occur. First, you are literally arguing with God by stating that what has happened should not have happened. You are telling the universe that you feel *you know* what should have happened, although you have no knowledge of any bigger picture from a universal perspective. Free will is a God-given attribute that all humans have, and it is what we all came here to experience. That is why everything the collective creates is allowed to happen. It is a learning experience for all of us from a connected, spiritual perspective.

Second, when you judge something or think about it, you are giving it energy, which extends it into the future. If you are trying to avoid getting sick or want to recover from an illness, the last thing you should do is keep extending the problem into your future by continually judging it.

Let's review how this works by looking at a situation that is reported in the media. For example: an event takes place, which ends up being judged as something negative. A lot of social media follows, with more judgments being meted out as thousands weigh in on what took place. Do any of these judgments put out the fire and change the unhappy event into something positive? No – the opposite happens. People take stands, and more judgment follows. More fuel is added to the fire.

Even though this is how people try to influence others to side with them, to ostensibly undo the negative event and put an end to it, what they are really doing is making sure their desired outcome *does not occur.* Why? Because their judgments are broadcasting the same frequency as the negative event, in the hopes of getting a different outcome. However, all judgment extends the problem into the future by matching its frequency; it never solves it. This is the law of attraction at work.

Understand that the holographic universe does not judge; it mirrors back what your energy field is putting out. But because we were never taught that, we keep judging and find ourselves wondering why we need to address the same issues over and over. We do not understand that we are adding fuel to the fire and allowing it to continue. Furthermore, we are typically looking for a solution that lies outside of ourselves, as though we play no part in the creation of the problem. In truth, the answer to a problem will manifest when everyone contributing to its frequency stops emitting that same frequency. As Einstein put it, "We cannot solve our problems with the same thinking we used when we created them."

To affect positive change, the frequency of the solution must be higher than that of the problem. This can only occur by stepping back and accepting the problem, thought, or event. Just observe it. That means shifting into neutral, or "zero point" energy. The next step is to pivot by telling the universe, "I accept this because it has manifested. However, this does not serve me.

I choose to see love instead." By envisioning love and giving it intense focus, you are now putting out high-vibration energy. In doing this, the holographic universe will send back people and events of a higher frequency.

The takeaway is that when you control your own vibration, you are controlling everything that impacts you. As you keep doing this, you are changing energetic timelines; you are moving into a higher frequency, an alternate universe in which the problem can be solved. You will know you are there when you see that progress to solve the problem is being made. It is always by adding love to the mix that you can transform an old problem and allow it to fade into nothingness.

This process of radical acceptance – the acceptance of "what is" before pivoting – is how spiritual masters solve problems. It is a revolutionary idea in our society, and certainly not one that most of us have ever considered making. We have been programmed in such a way that our egos are invested in placing blame outside of ourselves and insisting that someone else solve our problems for us. It is only when you get tired of the "same old, same old" that you will be open to change. When you are, it will be this process that gets real results.

When it comes to creating and maintaining good health, radical acceptance is what allows you to step away from fear, which includes all disease, and step up into love. That is most definitely what you want your life to be built on going forward.

Be the Captain of Your Ship

Right thinking for high-frequency health means accepting your power and using it. You acknowledge that you are not a victim. You are the creator of your life – the captain of your ship.

Instead of moving the deck chairs around on the *Titanic*, you are steering it in a new direction. Being powerful means standing in your light, knowing your purpose, and having faith that you are here for a reason that is loving. Instead of comparing yourself unfavorably to others, take stock of all your positive attributes. Then ask yourself, "What do I want to sow? What is my dream come true? Do I believe I have the power to get it?" This will tell you a lot about who you believe yourself to be and how powerful you think you are.

As often as we all unconsciously look to others to make things right for us, the fact is that no one is coming to save us. There is no prince on a white horse who will ride in to save the day. We need to get comfortable with the idea that we are perfectly capable of doing that for ourselves. That means we need to step into our own power and make it happen. Choose to see those around you with kindness and compassion. Try to offer words of loving support and encouragement in any way possible. Get used to seeing yourself standing in your own power and light!

When something no longer serves you, accept that it had its time and let it go. Then, focus on creating what you want. This is what it takes to be the powerful creator you really are – one who is capable of manifesting a sense of safety and peace. It is also how to raise your frequency and keep it high.

Your Emotional Guidance System

It takes discernment to make sound, loving decisions. Where should your guidance come from? Your emotional guidance system. It is your connection to the divine, your true North Star. How does it work? When you feel great, upbeat, and happy, you are on track and living your life's purpose. When you are not, you will feel it in the pit of your stomach and know you are off track. It is always 100 percent accurate at telling you whether you are in or out of alignment with love. To understand its messages, you need to pay attention and trust your inner knowing.

We all have experiences that take us down. Typically, we handle them with internal self-talk that places the blame outside of ourselves. In our society, we are frequently told to "keep a stiff upper lip and keep going." But that is essentially saying, "Don't take the time to figure out what you just did. Ignore it and move on." In listening to that unloving guidance, you are never going to connect your fearful thoughts with the situation they created for you. The same experience will happen again because you are not looking inside; you are not stopping the problem at its root.

If you are making someone else guilty for something and trying to solve a problem with denial and anger, you are in for more negativity and no resolution. Your projection, which makes another person guilty, is always an effort to absolve yourself of any guilt and feel better about a low-frequency belief you are harboring. The way to turn around all misunderstandings that result from judgment is by listening to what your emotional guidance system tells you. It will come to you as a feeling that is either positive or negative. Take time to step back and assess your thoughts. How do they make you feel? If you are unhappy and insecure, it is a sure sign that you judged something and that the judgment you made is incorrect.

As I go through my day, I am constantly assessing whether I am on track and high vibe. When I feel a pit in my stomach or my positive energy declining, I immediately revisit the thoughts I had prior to experiencing that sinking feeling. It always leads me to thoughts of resistance or judgment about myself; typically, it is one that tells me I am not good enough. When you get to that point, what is the next step? Forgiveness.

The Frequency of Forgiveness

There is no doubt that every day we are on this earth, we can find something to forgive. We live in a realm in which love does not seem to be "all that is." This is a world where we can experience opposites; good and bad, light and dark. It is a state of duality rather than unity with Source. In this realm, we are given the free will to experience that which we are not, so that we may come to understand more fully that which we truly are. You can better appreciate the good once you experience the bad.

With so much negativity being manifested by the collective, there is no shortage of anything to use as a forgiveness experience. But it is important to define forgiveness. Why? Because true forgiveness, which sets you free, is not generally what the world believes forgiveness to be. As I was growing up, I was always taught to forgive the other person. That was the thing to do because the other person was viewed as having done something wrong and needed to be forgiven for doing it. If I were being magnanimous, I could forgive what the other did, but my forgiveness did not wipe out the sin. I was merely letting the other person know that I was deciding to see the sin as unimportant. I also want to state that I find most people do not want to forgive anything or anyone. Their ego is determined to make the other person guilty and keep them there.

The frequency of forgiveness as practiced throughout the world today – is fairly low. It extends the "sin" into the future by judging the person as guilty for what they did even though they can be let off the hook by someone being "holier than thou." In truth, seeing anyone as guilty is just another judgment of self and not actual forgiveness of the other.

True Forgiveness

True forgiveness takes a different approach to sin: it says there is none. This forgiveness is a spiritual practice that you will only use when you are ready to stop judging and condemning others, in order to make yourself feel superior. Why? With true forgiveness, no one is guilty. It acknowledges our true nature is as spirit and we remain that way.

True forgiveness rests on the truth that our experience here in the physical realm is an illusion – a dream of separation from

Source. Because it is impossible to be separate from the Creator, when you forgive someone using the true forgiveness practice, you are acknowledging that this is all a dream and, therefore, nothing ever occurred. Source remains "All That Is," and you see the other as the perfect child of God they truly are and join with them in peace. That release from sin is high frequency because it is completely loving. It is also quantum because as it sees only love, it collapses time by healing on all levels, across all time. If you choose to practice this type of forgiveness, you will heal all thoughts of disease, because that frequency is simply incompatible with the frequency of pure love.

Step into Your Own Power

Once you are committed to changing your mind and leaving the fear of disease behind, you will step into your own power. As you change your mind about who you are and what you are capable of in life, you are choosing love over fear. This raises your frequency so high that you will never worry about being sick. Love's energies heal everything. That is why it is important to take the time to root out old beliefs and thoughts that are keeping you down in the battlefield of fear. If you built up hate and anger toward another, you must spend time looking deep within yourself to identify the cause and turn it around. Forgiveness of "other" is always forgiveness of self, so doing the work is one of the healthiest things you can do, because it is loving.

Here is the real secret: nothing ever heals you except you. Healers outside of you temporarily remove the problem but they do not heal it. No matter what regimen, pill, or process you undertake to heal from an illness or prevent an illness, the only way to be truly healthy is for you to stop thinking and believing whatever low frequency thoughts and beliefs brought the problem to you in the first place. When you understand that, you will be able to be the powerful, perfectly healthy creator you really are.

Avoid setting yourself up for a life that is less than what you are capable of living. Marlon Brando's famous performance in *On the Waterfront* and his line "I coulda been a contender" was one of the highlights of his career. However, your choice to mimic the life of that character and play small is never going to give you the life you came to lead.

Open your heart to the love you are, and know you are always loved beyond all measure. This life is so valuable. When you exist in a constant state of abundant love, good health, and happiness, you do not fear *anything*. Once that is the case, it is easy to take responsibility for yourself and practice the self-care you need to remain healthy. You honor the body that gets you through the day, year after year. You are grateful for every opportunity to be alive on this planet, sharing your unique gifts with the world. When night falls and you think back on how blessed you are to have the experiences you have, sit quietly and give thanks for the magnificence of your journey back to wholeness and the life that you can now live beyond disease.

Remember, you came here to experience a fully realized life. Throw limitations to the wind and step into your energy to become fully empowered. Feel yourself energized by, and enthusiastic about, life. When you forgive yourself for being weak, unworthy, unloving, and unlovable, oceans of opportunity that were previously unavailable to you, because of your low frequency, will show up for you. That is when you can build the life you always wanted and were determined to create from the start.

Exercise: True Forgiveness

You can do the exercise below for as many people as you like, going through the prayer for each one, day after day. If you feel a lot of anger toward someone, it will take many forgiveness exercises to let your anger go. That is normal. The good news is that you are committed to turning around your anger and healing. I find that as soon as I feel upset when I think about someone, I understand that I need to forgive them for something they *did not do*. I always end my prayer by envisioning myself giving them a hug and telling them that I love them.

This forgiveness process comes from Gary Renard, who wrote *The Disappearance of the Universe*. It comes from his ascended masters, and I use my own version of it every day as I go through my day. Every time I have an unloving thought about someone or feel off track, I immediately practice this prayer, no matter where I am – at my desk, out to lunch, or at a conference. It does not matter.

It takes a lot of forgiving to let go of your issues with anyone – some much more so than others. If you are serious about raising your frequency, you will adopt this form of forgiveness and spend the rest of your life putting it to good use. You will end up much happier and healthier because of it.

Begin your true forgiveness by thinking of someone you need to forgive. This will be the person who keeps showing up in your mind as a negative; the one you dream of telling off or are constantly doing battle within your mind. With a view of them front and center in your mind's eye, mentally tell them, "You are not really there. If I think you are guilty or the cause of the problem and I made you up, then the imagined guilt and fear are my own. Since the separation from God never really occurred, I forgive both of us for what never really happened. Now, there is only innocence and I join with the Holy Spirit in peace."

End by telling the person, "You are divine: loving and innocent. All is forgiven and released. You are divine: loving and innocent. All is forgiven and released. You are divine: loving and innocent. All is forgiven and released."

CHAPTER 9

CREATING A HIGH-FREQUENCY LIFESTYLE

E ach and every day, make it a point to begin your routine by reminding yourself of how great you are and how beautiful your life is. Take a few moments to appreciate all that surrounds you. You might start by enjoying the morning light that filters through the window and lights up the room. Breathe in the rich aroma of the coffee that is brewing. Watch your animals play. Admire the art you placed on your walls. Be grateful for the softness of the carpet beneath your feet. Enjoy your breakfast. If you are with your loved ones, let them know you love them and are happy to be with them. Look outside and give thanks for the natural world. Feel your appreciation open your heart and enjoy the moment.

Make every second of every day the gift you give yourself by giving thanks for all that you have in your world. This is the powerful you, affirming your ability to create a peaceful, loving, healthy life. What happens on an energetic level when you shift your focus into a higher vibration? The energetic vortices of your cells open up like flowers blossoming on a sunny day as you tune into the vibrations of well-being, happiness, peace, joy, and love. When you project that vibrational frequency to the universe, that is what will be returned to you.

Love the Life You Are Creating

To create a high-frequency life, use the first several minutes after waking up to set your intentions for the day from a place of positivity and power. Ask for guidance so that whatever happens that day, you will be able to handle it with ease and confidence. As you move through your day, take a minute every hour to express gratitude for the people, places, and events in your life. Use each moment to be as consciously positive as possible. Tell yourself that everything is exactly as it should be in that moment. If you do want to see something become more loving, accept the situation for how it shows up. Then, pivot by stating it no longer serves you and reframe it by adding love to the mix.

Once you can be radically accepting and nonjudgmental of what concerns you, and you pivot by envisioning a loving outcome, end with the thought, "And so it is." Each time a negative thought arises, tell yourself that it had its part to play, and it is over. Never waste any time or energy in an argument with yourself or anyone else. It merely leads to lower frequencies being extended into the future.

If you are on edge and uncertain of how to proceed, how can you raise your frequency and let go of the fear? Take a minute to ask for guidance and sit quietly to clear your mind. When you can, write down your thoughts in your Discovery Journal and turn around any that are negative. Remember, if you are off track, you judged someone or something. Identify what the judgment was and then tell yourself that the story you believed was untrue. Forgive it and let it go by using the true forgiveness prayer.

Lifestyle Matters

How you live your life impacts your frequency. It goes without saying that if you smoke, drink more than a glass or two of alcohol per day, or do drugs, your vibrational frequency could be below 62 Hz. To minimize any damage you are doing to your physical body and prevent the development of a disease such as cancer, it is in your interest to overcome your addiction as quickly as possible.

Living a healthy, high-vibe life will be easier when you are fully present and mindful of what you are thinking. We are living in high-energy times, and your ability to adjust and adapt to any energy fluctuation in the world is dependent on your ability to remain nonjudgmental and focused on the present. A great way to teach yourself how to go through life with this vibration is by meditating.

Meditation

Meditation allows you to slow down, listen, and connect with your inner guidance. Few things are better at helping you relax than this practice. Begin each meditation by focusing on your breath. Take a deep breath on a count of five. Hold it for five seconds, and then release it on a count of five. Do this three times.

If you are new to meditation, you may find that it is difficult to quiet your mind. When that happens, imagine yourself sitting on a park bench, watching people walk by. Those individuals are your thoughts. Just observe them as they move. At some point, you will relax into silence. Arriving at this stillness is how you train yourself to be an observer of situations and events in your life. Over time, you will find that you are completely able to be calm and centered in the midst of any discord.

Another way to approach meditation is to become laser-focused in the present with your intention. This means you tune in completely to what you are involved in. This type of meditation is great to use when you are out and about in the world and need to forgive something or someone. Home in on whatever or whoever needs your forgiveness and then proceed with the true forgiveness prayer. Envision fully that which you want the outcome to be. Your focus, your envisioning, is the meditation. The power of your focus will determine the results.

Meditation is a most valuable tool for helping you navigate the frustrations and stresses of daily life: the traffic, irritating salespeople, or anything that pushes your buttons. In time, you will become proficient at stepping back, observing, and pivoting to a higher frequency when any challenge appears before you.

Creativity

Another way to raise your frequency is to do what you love to do. All creativity feeds your soul. If you love dancing, dance. If you enjoy singing, sing. If painting or drawing fulfills you, then do that. If it is cooking, then cook. Feed your inner artist and let your creations fill your world. Then share them with others. That is what makes life worth living!

When I had cancer, I had a reading with a psychic who told me that one of the reasons my energy was low was because I was not being creative. To raise my frequency, I was to do something creative every day. She then added that if I continued resisting my creativity, it was only a matter of time before the disease would spread. Needless to say, no doctor ever prescribed being creative as part of my journey back to wellness.

How did I respond? I bought colored pencils and a coloring book and began to color. I started playing more with my dogs and talking to my plants. I began singing along to the radio while driving. I bought a camera and began to take pictures of beautiful sunrises. I started practicing my automatic writing. In short, I added joy to my life by doing little things that made me happy.

Love Your Relationships

It goes without saying that to achieve and maintain a high frequency, you need to be loving. Your family, friends, and animals are the most obvious loves of your life. Make it a point to see them all through loving eyes. Be kind and compassionate. Be patient and listen to others. Stop trying to control anyone else and focus on staying in your own swim lane. You are here to live life to the fullest. Relax, enjoy each day, and be grateful for your time with all those who share your life, including your animals. They are why you came.

Love Your Body

It is impossible to have a healthy life if your thoughts about yourself are not loving. Disease originates with the thousands of negative thoughts you had about yourself over a long period of time. Many of these beliefs and thoughts are centered on our bodies. How often do you look in the mirror and find something to criticize? We are constantly thinking about how good we do or do not look, how fat or thin we are, and how old-looking or young-looking we appear. All of this is egoic and unhealthy. Look in the mirror and tell yourself how wonderful you look, how healthy you are, and how radiant and beautiful you are. Your task is to love yourself truly and unconditionally.

Complement your positive self-talk by practicing loving self-care. This starts with good nutrition. Make it a point to eat a diet of as many high-frequency foods as possible. Buy fruits and vegetables that are organically farmed. If you eat meat, purchase it from a local butcher who can tell you where the animal was raised and how it was fed. Make sure the fish you eat is never farm-raised or one that is over-fished.

Make exercise a regular part of your day. It tones your muscles and helps you maintain an appropriate weight, improve your outlook on life, minimize stress, and prevent disease. Establish a weekly routine and stick to it. Working out with light weights, strength training, and stretching are great for toning. If you enjoy yoga or Pilates, make those a part of your routine. Aerobics and dance build stamina, and balance work keeps you steady on your feet.

Be proactive when it comes to your health. Visit your medical doctor for a yearly checkup. If you are female and over thirty-five, get a yearly mammogram. In addition to benefiting from what Western medicine has to offer, you might want to consider integrating alternative therapies into your routine. Reiki, massage, and acupuncture may all be helpful. If you are interested in having any energy work done to clear blockages, consider having regular biofield tune-ups.

To make sure you get the rest you need, establish a schedule for your sleep by turning out the lights and setting the alarm for the same time every day. Make sure your bedroom is dark and eat early enough in the evening so that you do not go to sleep right after eating. Never go to bed with the television on.

Reduce Radiation Hazards in Your Environment

In today's high-tech world, we are constantly exposed to radiation from electric and magnetic fields (EMFs). These are invisible areas of energy that are associated with the use of electrical power and various forms of natural and man-made lighting. Radiation of any kind is not good for your health. Exposure to EMFs, in particular, is associated with health concerns that include abnormal cell growth, nerve cell damage, infertility, immune system dysfunction and sleep disturbances. EMFs are typically grouped into one of two categories by their frequency:

- Non-ionizing: Low-level radiation, which is generally perceived as harmless to humans
- Ionizing: High-level radiation, which has the potential for cellular and DNA damage

Sources of non-ionizing EMFs include:

- Radio and television signals
- Televisions, computer screens, and tablets
- Radar, satellite stations, magnetic resonance imaging (MRI) devices, and industrial equipment
- Microwave ovens
- Cell phones
- Wireless local area networks (Wi-Fi)

To raise your frequency and keep radiation in your home and work environment to a minimum, you need to distance yourself from these devices and use them only when necessary. For example, when using your microwave, walk into another room. Before you go to bed at night, turn off your cell phone or place it in a different room. If you are using it as an alarm, switch it to airplane mode so it emits no signal.

What can you do to reduce any adverse effects from exposure to EMFs in your home? Minimize your use of EMF-generating technologies. To do that, turn off your Wi-Fi at night, limit the amount of time you spend watching television, and limit your cell phone use. You may also want to stop using your microwave altogether.

You might also consider purchasing devices that block EMFs. If you search the internet for EMF shielding devices, you will see that this marketplace is thriving. In performing your search, you will be able to find any number of products to suit you, including cell phone discs, computer strips, ear buds, bracelets, pendants, and other items that purport to turn EMFs into bio-compatible electro-magnetic healing fields. With so many protective products to choose from, do your research to ensure the product is safe and has been vetted before making your purchase.

Finally, add plants to your home. In 1989, NASA studied whether plants reduce air pollution onboard the International Space Station. Over the years, their studies proved that plants are effective at reducing air pollution, and some are also good at absorbing EMFs. One of the most effective at doing this is the cactus, but there is no doubt that others can also be helpful at reducing the radioactivity in your home and office.

Love Mother Earth

We live on a beautiful planet, so take advantage of that by spending time in Mother Nature. Nothing raises your frequency like being out in the sun. Just be sure to wear a brimmed hat in the summer and cover your skin to protect yourself from sunburn. If you have the time and are in good enough physical shape, go for a hike. Another option is to read a book or write in your journal while sitting under a tree. If nothing else, take a ten-minute walk in the morning and evening. Be sure to walk in shoes without rubber soles. Rubber prevents your body from grounding with the earth, so wear leather-soled shoes to connect with Earth's energy and raise your frequency.

Treat the planet well by showing her love and respect. Be thoughtful in your purchases so you reduce the amount of plastic you use. As energetic beings, we are connected to everything in our world. Understand that the frequency of the care you give to the planet is what will be returned to you in full measure, so be as loving to Mother Nature as you can be.

Music that Heals

Music plays such an important role in our lives. While all types of music can be enjoyed, certain ones are more beneficial to our health than others. At the top of the list are Gregorian chants and Indian Sanskrit chants. Why are they worth listening to? They contain tones that resonate at certain frequencies known as Solfeggio tones – a series of electromagnetic sound frequencies that are reputed to date back hundreds, if not thousands of years. They were rediscovered by Dr. Joseph Puleo, an American naturopath who used them to correct imbalances in his patients' bodies in the 1970s.

Puleo's work was followed by research that was undertaken by a biochemist named Dr. Glen Rein, who tested the impact of music on human DNA. In the late 1980s, he determined that Gregorian and Sanskrit chants, both of which incorporate Solfeggio tones in almost all their songs, increased ultraviolet (UV) light absorption in humans between 5 and 9 percent. Classical music increased UV absorption by small amounts, and rock music decreased UV light absorption and harmed DNA. Rein's research supported the long-held theory that sound frequencies do affect human health.

Since Rein's work, further research has confirmed that Solfeggio tones have profound mental, emotional, and physical effects. This has led to music therapy becoming a respected therapy for treating a variety of health issues. Today, the most popular form of music that uses the tones consistently is known as "New Age," and almost all music composed for meditation and relaxation includes at least some of these tones. The six Solfeggio tones that correspond to do, re, mi, fa, sol, and la are:

- 396 Hz – Music tuned to this frequency removes subconscious fears, worries, and anxiety. It also eliminates feelings of guilt and subconscious negative beliefs blocking the path to achieving personal goals. It is ideal to listen to music of this frequency when you want to feel uplifted, secure, and empowered.

- 432 Hz – Music tuned to this frequency makes you feel peaceful and in a state of well-being. It is an ideal background for yoga, meditation, or sleep.
- 528 Hz – Music tuned to this frequency significantly reduces stress in the endocrine and autonomic nervous system.
- 639 Hz – Music tuned to this frequency balances emotions and elevates mood. It is ideal to listen to this when you want a boost of love and positivity or are trying to resolve conflict.
- 741 Hz – Music tuned to this frequency is good for helping you to cleanse your body, upgrade to a healthier lifestyle, and live simply. It also helps you develop intuition, express creativity, and speak your truth.
- 852 Hz – Music tuned to this frequency helps you replace negative thoughts with positive ones and live your highest self.

Exercise: Mindful Meditation

Sit quietly and comfortably. When you are relaxed, close your eyes and envision yourself entering a garden full of colorful flowers and lush vegetation. A shallow brook babbles just ahead. Butterflies and hummingbirds flit delicately in the air around you. Find a bench and sit down to enjoy the serenity of the environment.

Tell yourself, "I am healthy, healed, and whole." Relax and enjoy the warmth of the sun shining down on your back. Listen to the water flowing gently over rocks in the stream. It is good to be in the garden where all is exactly as it should be, and you are as you are meant to be in this time and space. Breathe in the sweetness of the air. You are powerful, calm, and collected. Rest in your positivity and power.

Spend as much time there as you like, quietly giving thanks for all the blessings in your life. When you are ready, open your eyes and state out loud, "I am thankful to be healthy, healed, and whole. I am a powerful creative who can lead a disease-free life. Namaste."

CHAPTER 10

LIFE ABOVE THE FREQUENCY OF DISEASE

s it possible to never get sick in your life? Absolutely. But the irony is that you will not achieve that by focusing on the body. It results from a mind which is healed and in alignment with love. Mastery of the mind *is* mastery of the body. If you want to stay healthy, cultivate a connection to the divine. It is about understanding that everyone is an aspect of you and that it is pointless to judge. In fact, judgment is what can take you down to the frequency of disease. I understand that quite well because I lived it. It was only when I examined what was going on in my mind and started to forgive my negative beliefs that I was able to get healthy and live at a frequency above disease.

Self-Care Routine for Good Health

The saying "without your health, you have nothing" is not far from the truth. When I had cancer the first time and was undergoing chemotherapy infusions, all I wanted was to have my good health back. I wanted my hair and eyesight back, and I wanted my body to work so that I could take a long walk, go up a flight of steps without losing my breath, and stand up without needing to sit back down. I wanted to move as effortlessly as I had before my treatments began. I wanted to think clearly and have my memory return.

Cancer is a life-changing disease, and it certainly impacted me physically, mentally, and emotionally. My hair never fully grew back. My joints are still a problem. I still have a poor memory and need to wear glasses. But the silver lining is that I am a much stronger person emotionally. I am kinder, more empathetic, and more caring. I upgraded my view of the world and understand the value of everyone who lives on this planet with me. I also developed a routine that not only helps me physically but mentally, spiritually, and emotionally. I follow it every day to the best of my ability, and I firmly believe it helps me remain high frequency and, therefore, immune to disease.

Here are my suggestions for a self-care routine that are helping me live at a frequency above disease:

- Begin your day with a prayer of thanks. Start this just as you wake up, before getting out of bed. Give thanks for the guidance that you will receive throughout the day, and commit to spending your time without fear, resentment, or judgment.
- Look at yourself in the mirror and tell yourself how wonderful, kind, and loving you are.
- Drink an eight-ounce glass of filtered water before drinking anything else.
- Get outside for at least a ten-minute morning walk or run.
- Eat a breakfast that includes high fiber, protein, and as many vitamins and minerals as possible.
- Set aside ten to fifteen minutes for a morning meditation, either before or after breakfast.
- If you commute to a job, use that time to give thanks for the creative opportunities and love that will come your

way. Be thankful for the opportunity to be of service to others, yourself, and the highest good.

- Eat a lunch that includes as many fresh fruits and vegetables as possible.
- Snack on raw nuts and a piece of fruit.
- Drink filtered water throughout the day instead of caffeinated beverages.
- Do not engage in gossip or negative conversations about others.
- Focus on being fully present.
- Think loving thoughts.
- Get outside for a ten-minute walk every afternoon or early evening, if possible.
- Make a note of any thoughts that trigger you during the day. Write them down in your Discovery Journal when you get home. Spend the time it takes to identify the root belief that needs to be replaced. Replace the unhealthy belief by acknowledging that it no longer serves you. Write down a loving thought to replace it and read it out loud.
- If you watch television, make sure the program is nonviolent and uplifting. Anything else will take down your frequency, so be selective about what you watch as entertainment.
- Do not indulge in any entertainment that is violent or disrespectful to others or yourself.
- Meditate for ten to fifteen minutes before going to bed.
- Turn off your electronic devices and Wi-Fi before going to bed.
- Once you are in bed, give thanks for your day. Ask for guidance so that the messages you receive while you sleep are remembered and understood.

Essential Oils

In researching everything I could do to maintain a healthy immune system, I noticed articles about essential oils. When I delved a bit further into why they are so popular, what became clear is that research confirms their health benefits. Gary Young, the founder of Young Living Essential Oils, worked with Bruce Tainio to measure the frequency of essential oils. What they discovered was astounding. As Gary relates in his book, *Aromatherapy: The Essential Beginning*, the measured frequencies of the oils began at 52 Hz (the frequency of basil oil) and went as high as 320 Hz (the frequency of rose oil).

Essential oils can clear negative energy in a space and raise the vibration of the people within it. Some of the best for this purpose are lavender, sage, lemongrass, jasmine, frankincense, patchouli, myrrh, cedarwood, juniper, and rose. I use rose oil every day, rubbing it into my wrists and inhaling its scent throughout the day. It makes me feel calm and centered.

Below is a list of some essential oils and their associated frequency.

Rose (*Rosa damascene*)	320 Hz
Frankincense	147 Hz
Lavender (*Lavendula angustifolia*)	118 Hz
Myrrh (*Commiphora myrrha*)	105 Hz
Blue Chamomile (*Matricaria recutita*)	105 Hz
Juniper (*Juniperus osteosperma*)	98 Hz
Aloes/Sandalwood (*Santalum album*)	96 Hz
Angelica (*Angelica archangelica*)	85 Hz
Peppermint (*Mentha peperita*)	78 Hz
Galbanum (*Ferula gummosa*)	56 Hz
Basil (*Ocimum basilicum*)	52 Hz

Thrive!

There are few feelings more uplifting than owning your power. It is so self-affirming and positive to stand in your own light. It is as if you are "on fire." The more you think positive, the more frequently you will experience this state of being. When you devote your entire day to being mindful and fully present, forgiving the thoughts that are low frequency, and being loving toward yourself and all others, your life will become so high frequency that you will truly be "unstoppable." You are a sacred, eternal being and are connected to everything that exists. Use your power right here, right now, to envision a beautiful, healthy world. When you use each moment to create the most uplifting world you can imagine, rest assured that your future will be bright, loving, and healthy.

Choose Once Again

You may have heard the quote, "The definition of insanity is doing the same thing over and over again and expecting different results." It is the perfect example of how you cannot solve any problem by expecting the beliefs and frequency that brought the condition or event *to* you to solve it *for* you. The physical world is the result of past thoughts, so do not look to any old way of thinking or long-held belief for your answer to any problem. Turn your focus inward to explore what you are thinking now. By changing any negative thoughts into ones that are loving, your experience of the physical world cannot help but be brought into alignment with love, which is the highest frequency there is. Be vigilant in seeing only the higher-frequency thoughts. Those will resolve your problems. They are waiting for you in an energetic field of pure potentiality. The instant your frequency becomes a match to them, they can manifest for you. Remember, all challenges are merely opportunities to choose once again and reap a different, and hopefully higher-frequency, result.

Individuals Who Overcame Disease

I know it is possible to overcome disease at any stage, even if death seems imminent. The choice for good health is always an option until you choose otherwise. Do I know people who brought themselves back from the brink of death? Yes. How about those who were cured from cancer and have never had a recurrence? Most certainly. My life is full of individuals who overcame and continue to overcome extreme health issues.

What do they all have in common? A will to live, a positive attitude, an interest in creativity, and a competitive spirit. They all accept the challenges before them and never let any of it hold them back from accomplishing what they came to do. None of them ever complained about their lot in life. They know they make a difference and are living large.

Susan was born with two holes in her heart. She was one of the first children in the country to have the corrective surgery for the condition. Susan has gone on to lead a normal life, have a career, get married, and raise a large family.

June was born with a tumor on her spine. The operation to remove it when she was two years old led to the development of severe scoliosis and a host of other problems. Despite any setback, she has enjoyed an impressive career and never let anything hold her back. Although she has had over ten surgeries in the last several years alone, she is still working and enjoying her life.

Ira developed breast cancer when he was in his fifties. After having a lumpectomy and undergoing chemo and radiation, he went right back to producing television shows. Twenty years later, with most of his peers fully retired, he is still doing what he loves to do: producing public television programs that educate and entertain.

John was diagnosed with Stage 4 colon cancer in his early fifties. After being given three months to live, he went on to coach his young son's football team and won state championships year after year.

Katie was diagnosed with Stage 3 breast cancer in her early thirties. At the time, she admitted she had lived in dread of getting cancer, as her mother and grandmother did. With three children under the age of six, she had a lot to live for. Katie became committed to turning around all the negatives in her life: her stressful job, her worries as a parent, and her long-standing belief in illness. She began taking time to do one of the things she loved to do most: ride horses. She also made it a point to prepare healthy, beautiful meals for her family and began to put her own needs first. The result is that although roughly 30 percent of all cancer survivors experience a recurrence; she never has. Twenty-five years later, her children are grown, her marriage is happy, she has a career she loves, and she still makes time to go riding. In short, she cultivated a habit of living on the bright side of life and stopped letting her beliefs in her own powerlessness make her sick.

I could go on, but I think you get the picture. The point is that life is what you make it. Stop complaining and commit to being positive. Set your sights high and never look back. Choose to live fearlessly every moment of each day and keep blazing your trail forward!

Exercise: The Frequency of Love

Sit quietly and observe your world. Give thanks for the moment and then tell yourself, "I give thanks for [whatever you are appreciating]." Continue with the following prayer of gratitude:

"I give thanks for all the hands and hearts that contributed to this moment and brought this into my life. I give thanks for the spirit of love within me that connects me to all that is in this moment and eternally. I give thanks for the spirit of love that lives and breathes in me now."

Close your eyes. Breathe deeply and slowly. Envision your

gratitude and love filling every cell of your body and expanding outward as a beautiful light, radiating from you and blessing all who are nearby. Watch as your heart opens and your love extends throughout your neighborhood, your region, your country, and the world. Watch as the world turns, encircled by your radiant love and gratitude.

When you are ready, come back to your body and go about your day peacefully and joyfully.

CHAPTER 11

OVERCOMING A DIP IN FREQUENCY

In today's world, it is easy to experience a dip in frequency. Just as the pollution on our planet is a huge health hazard, so are negative thoughts. Everything we think, say, and do affects our body's frequency. Everything we consume does as well. We all start out our days with good intentions, but it can take only an instant to get off track if we do not focus on being positive.

What becomes clear is that you must make a commitment to being aware and focused if you are to stay in alignment with positivity and maintain a high frequency. You also understand that it can be just as challenging to remain healthy as it is to get healthy. If you are not taking care of yourself holistically, you will not live the life you desire, nor will you have the love you want to share with others. Mental, emotional, and physical self-care is the answer. Make a commitment to yourself that you will put your health first so you can enjoy the life you want to live.

Do Right by Your Body

Love the skin you are in. Remember that saying? It is worth repeating. You need to maintain the vehicle that allows you to get around this world and live your beautiful life. Just as a car needs periodic maintenance, so does a body. Too often, we put off going to the doctor until a situation is serious. If you are one of those people, turn that around. The sooner you take care of any physical problem, the easier it is to solve. Make it a point to have regular physicals, especially as you age.

Are you exercising? If not, it is time to start. Physical exercise not only supports your good health; it determines your frequency. So, make time for it, no matter how tired you are. Instead of being a couch potato for hours on end, take a walk, go hiking, or bike around your neighborhood. When you are done, ground your body by planting your bare feet on the earth. The more you get back to including Mother Nature in your daily routine, the less likely it will be that you slip down into a frequency you should have left for good.

Look at your diet. Did you eat fast food this week? Is it still one of your standard meals? We all lead busy lives, and many of us start the day with a protein bar and caffeinated drink. Lunch is grab and go, and dinner is frequently takeout. It is a good bet that none of that is high frequency.

Going rogue with your diet is okay if it is only once in a blue moon. Enjoy a piece of birthday cake when you attend a party. By no means should you spend the end of year holidays in a funk because you are denying yourself your favorite glass of wine or a rich meal with friends and family. Go watch a sporting event and have a hot dog or burger. Life is to be enjoyed. But after you binge, get back in the saddle and eat healthy.

Be the Sovereign Being You Were Born to Be

If you let others' opinions of who you are, what you should be thinking, what you should be doing, or how you should be living take precedence over what you want to do and how you want to live, you will not attain a high-frequency life. Why?

Because you are telling the universe you are powerless. Start to acknowledge that you are a sovereign being and take responsibility for everything in your life. Stop caring about others' judgments; stand up for yourself, your creativity, desires, and beliefs. Step into your own power by speaking your truth, acknowledging your purpose and living fearlessly with love and compassion.

Be Your Own Medical Advocate

Do not ingest any drug prescribed by a doctor or the medical community without knowing what the ingredients, side effects, and potential risks are. As I learned firsthand over the course of my disease, big pharmaceutical companies do not care about your health. They are profit and control oriented. You must use the utmost discernment in deciding what drugs to take and for how long. If you do not care enough to be your own medical advocate, find someone who will advocate on your behalf. To be high frequency, you need to be proactive when it comes to your health, not reactive.

Stop the Judgment

When life gets stressful and things do not "roll out" the way you thought they would or should, you are judging. Running negative stories about yourself and others, insisting that others bend to your rules because you know best, and projecting fearful outcomes for a whole host of scenarios are all low-frequency behaviors. The ego is always interested in conflict and drama. However, you will never achieve or maintain a healthy life if you choose to feed your ego rather than undo it. Stop expecting everything be what you decide is acceptable and correct. Open yourself up to seeing that many roads lead to Rome. It is not about being right. It is about being loving.

Stop Resisting Change

Fear has a way of showing up as resistance, especially when it comes to changing the way you have been living your life: the things you think, the things you say, what you do, how you eat, and how you manage your way through each day. It is this fear that causes blocks in your energy field. They are created as you begin to doubt yourself, doubt that you are powerful, and doubt that good health can be a constant.

You may have started the process to change up your world, and felt it is not happening fast enough. Quit second guessing yourself. The more you resist, the more negativity you will be broadcasting as a low frequency vibration across the universe. That can literally block the positive supporting vibrations around you and can have unhealthy consequences. When you feel off in any way, know that you could be creating this kind of a block. Take time to reflect on your fears and frustrations and allow yourself more time to make the changes that you set out to make. Keep replacing unhealthy thoughts with affirmations as quickly as possible. If necessary, book a session with an energy healer. Above all, make true forgiveness your go-to practice for overcoming any negativity.

Be Fully Present

Few things take down your frequency more quickly than a constant replay of the past. Every time you go back into the past to relive an old hurt by someone else, you are hurting yourself again – and each time, you are doing it to yourself. Stop that behavior immediately. Forgive the old hurt and concentrate on being fully present.

Focus on the present and what you want your life to be. If you need to heal a relationship with someone, quit envisioning the former negativity you experienced and see yourself happy and content with that person. Understand that everyone appears in your life for a reason, and the reason is so that they can demonstrate to you a belief that *you* need to release. The faster you realize that and let old wounds go, the faster you can heal and create an exciting future.

Quiet Your Mind

If your mind is never at rest and you have a constant stream of self-doubting, internal talk going on, you will not be able to master your mind or body. Insecurity, guilt, and a sense of unworthiness are at play. Quit telling yourself these stories. Stop imagining yourself or someone else getting sick or having an accident. When you do that, you are inviting low frequency energy into your world. Learn to relax and quiet your mind. Meditate!

Listen to Your Emotional Guidance System

Do you find yourself ignoring the little voice that tells you to go one way and you deliberately go another? Stop discounting the information you receive from your inner self. You have a guidance system that is impeccable, and it constantly tells you when you are on and off track. If you are worried, anxious, or afraid, you are making judgments that are incorrect. Perhaps you have had fearful thoughts about your partner, and the bad feeling in the midsection of your torso is reflecting that.

The more you choose to listen to what your body is telling you, the more you will read the feedback correctly. We usually think that we feel bad because of what someone else did to us, but your emotional guidance system is only ever concerned with you. If you feel bad about something, it is because you misread the situation, judged it, and are in error. Start trusting your gut.

Stop Blaming and Start Forgiving

There is no doubt that we all learned to blame others for everything that does not go the way we feel it should go. It is your ego's way of relieving your own guilt. However, it never works. What that does is increase your seeming separation from God – in essence, you are making God the guilty party. God is All That Is. When you project your guilt onto someone else, because that person is another aspect of you as well as a part of God, all you are doing is making both yourself and God guilty. Clearly, that is no way to resolve anything.

When someone does something that you do not approve of or that is hurtful, accept the situation and then silently say the true forgiveness prayer. In forgiving the other for what they never did (because this is an illusion), you are forgiven for the same thing (because you and the other are one). That is how to be free from any form of fear that manifests for you. If you choose not to forgive, the low frequency of the hurt that you are choosing to extend into the future is guaranteed to come back around again.

Find Reasons to be Positive

Despite your good intentions, it is all too easy to stop seeing the positive in life and start believing that the world is going to hell in a hand basket. You stop remembering to see everyone as another aspect of you and start believing you have enemies. You see hate, evil and injustice "out there." You see everything that should not be allowed. The world is wrong, politicians are wrong, other people are wrong. That may be. But if you do not change those sentiments, you will never achieve or maintain a high-vibe life. You will have to live at the frequency of those sentiments.

When something triggers you into a feeling you do not like, ask yourself, "What thought can I think that feels better?" Look out the window. Breathe. Appreciate the beauty of the mountains in the distance, the color of the sky or the song of a bird in a tree. If you do not feel you can find anything in your view to focus on, meditate. Play a Gregorian chant and shift your focus by going inside. Once there, envision whatever makes you feel inspired and uplifted and go with the flow. Keep focusing on those feelings and raising your vibe. Imagine you are dialing a dial and tuning into higher and happier feelings. When you finish your meditation and you go back to thinking about your world, is all still lost? Or do you know deep inside that you have this?

When life gets you down, raise yourself up. This is the power of you. Live it by doing it. Take action to think yourself happier. Work on bringing up your confidence and your mood. If you give in to anger and discouragement, you are not helping yourself. Understand that with dedication you will create a beautiful life. It just takes a willingness to do it.

CHAPTER 12

MOVING POWERFULLY INTO
A HEALTHY FUTURE

All life is energy. It is everywhere and exists in everything. Every atom, molecule, cell, and tissue in your body is energetic. Every thought and feeling that you have is nothing but energy. The mass of your physical body combined with your thoughts and emotions create your personal energy field. This field is constantly vibrating and the vibration changes with each thought and feeling that you have, so although you were probably never told this, you can raise or lower your frequency at will.

Since the law of attraction applies to all energy, the frequency at which you project your energy field out into the universe is the same frequency of energy that the holographic universe will return to you. Like attracts like. That is why it is so important to maintain a high frequency. If you are healthy and are vibrating at a frequency between 62 and 78 Hz, the universe will send back energy that is of that healthy frequency.

While being loving raises your frequency and gives you access to higher realms where a healthier life is possible, all forms of fear – hatred, jealousy, envy, and revenge – resonate below 60

Hz. All disease, no matter what it is, vibrates at a frequency below the range of a healthy human body. In fact, viruses and unhealthy bacteria cannot exist at the frequency of good health. To prevent disease, understand that the most important component in creating good health comes from what you think. The mind is the builder. It is your subconscious mind that directs your body. The subconscious mind runs everything, so what you think matters. If you want to be healthy, you must think and feel your way to good health. If you realize that many of your thoughts are repetitively negative and that you are constantly seeing yourself and others as less than wonderful, stop. You will never be able to make any long-term changes in your life unless you address the beliefs that underlie your negative thoughts and behaviors.

Write down every unloving thought you have about yourself or someone else in your Discovery Journal. These must be acknowledged and then released through true forgiveness. Replace these judgments them with love. When you do, envision the brighter future you want for at least two minutes and feel its reality. With practice, you will be on your way to manifesting a better tomorrow.

Focus on the Frequency of Love

The frequency of pure love is the highest frequency there is. It is the frequency that heals. No matter what unloving thought you have, when you replace it with love, you can be healed. More importantly, by focusing on this frequency, you will heal yourself from any disease. Remember: all healing actually comes from within.

To focus on the frequency of love, get quiet. When your mind is still, you are relaxed and open to listening to guidance, so meditate on a regular basis. Clear away any thoughts that distract you by concentrating on your breathing. Inhale several deep breaths and slowly exhale them to calm yourself. Do this until you are fully relaxed. Then, just ask for guidance by talking directly to Source. This is done by opening your heart and sending out thoughts of love to yourself, your friends and family, your community, and the world.

In sending out energy at the frequency of love, and seeing love swirling around the planet, you are guaranteeing that love will return to you. Do this on a regular basis and you will raise your frequency to such a degree that your life will be full of grace.

Live in the Flow as the Captain of Your Ship

To live in the flow of grace, recognize that every moment of your life is what you make it. With every thought, word, and deed, you are the captain of your ship. If you focus on what you do not want to experience more of, you will energetically take it with you, because you are misusing the present moment to extend the past into the future. But if you focus with appreciation on what you learned, how you grew, and all the gifts of grace that emerged from your experiences, and you are grateful for it all, then the frequency of that gratitude is what you will experience in your future.

To live in the flow and better support the planet, eat fewer animal products. The healthiest diet for humans and the earth is one that is local, organic, and either vegetarian or vegan. Every move you make is either toward love or away from love, so be mindful of how your life impacts all life forms in the natural world. This is how you create a cleaner, more loving world in which cities have more greenery, people honor and respect all others, and nature restores balance. Believe in this, focus your energy on this, and it will come.

Be Powerfully, Joyfully Creative

As you move through your life, ask yourself, "Where am I lacking in creativity?" To be truly healthy, you must do what you love.

You must be passionate about your life and its creations. Do you need to dance more? Sing more? Grow a garden? Take photos? Write a book? What talents are you not using? What dreams are going unfulfilled for you?

Take back your life and stand in your power by being the creative force that you are. That is why you came to this planet: to create and live fully and fearlessly. So, do it. Be everything you came to be. That is how to live a joyful, amazing, and truly healthy life. Put away your phone and get out in nature. Stop worrying about getting sick or not having enough. Be abundant in your thoughts and your creativity and you will have everything your heart ever desired. Be the love and light you so desperately think waits for you outside of yourself. It comes from within. You will meet it when you project it. Be the powerful, loving, joyfully creative being that you truly are.

Choose a Life Above Disease

We are eternal energy beings – in essence, beings of light – who are experiencing life in human form. Because we are naturally creative, we each have the power to prevent disease by increasing the frequency of our bodies in order to defend against, and overcome, any illness.

To choose a life above disease, simply choose love each and every moment of every day. It is by being loving to yourself, to all others, and to the world that you ensure your health and vitality. What you reap is what you sow. Focus your thoughts by taking time to meditate and invoke the energies within you. Any disease can be eliminated by invoking more love into the world.

We are all here to bring about the change we want to have in the world. It will not come from outside of ourselves. All power to create is in the present moment and inside of us. When you clear your mind and vibrate in love and harmony with whatever you desire, it will be yours. If you find you are not positive enough to think the most loving thoughts, choose a feeling that is more loving, somewhere between where you find yourself now and where you want to be. For example, if you are worried, try focusing on moving up to contentment. Focus on feeling content until it brings you relief from your worry. When you feel up to it, find another emotion that makes you feel even better, perhaps optimism, and focus on being optimistic. Envision life through those rose-colored glasses for a day. If you keep this up, it will not take long before you work yourself up to the high vibe emotions you really want to experience all the time.

It is easy to get caught up in what is going on in the world outside of you and forget that the power you are looking for is within. But have faith in yourself and your abilities so that you can think healthy thoughts, raise your frequency, and access the powerfully creative and loving force that you are.

Understand that all disease is fear manifested in physical form. If you obsess about getting sick, you will be leaving yourself open to experience it. By focusing on love, you will experience more of it. As you do, you will find that where you used to be nervous, angry, and worried, you are now peaceful and confident. Each day you practice thinking positively will show you the true power of your mind.

When you retrain your mind to love unconditionally, nothing can prevent you from living the life you want and deserve. In allowing yourself to feel the love that is within you, you will be aligning with Source. It is just that simple and that amazing. So, remember to choose love – and live your life fully above the frequency of fear and disease.

ACKNOWLEDGMENTS

This book would never have been written without the care and guidance of Angela Lauria and her staff at The Author Incubator in Washington, DC. Thank you for helping me to make a difference in the world. I will always love you.

I am beyond grateful to my guides and teachers who helped me understand that every moment of this journey counts. Thank you for watching over me and shining the light ahead of me. You are, and will always be, the wings beneath my feet.

I give thanks to you, the person who picked up this book in hopes of overcoming a fear of death and disease. As a cancer survivor, I am thrilled to have the opportunity to continue living a healthy, joyous life. It was the thought of you that compelled me to share my story and I pray you join me in enjoying a life of great health and happiness. I know you now understand that your infinite power to create wellness lies in choosing love over fear. As we move further into the Age of Aquarius, I am certain we will continue helping others to achieve and maintain a high frequency that will hasten the heaven on Earth we are all waiting for – a world in which the darkness of fear is transformed into the light of love. Thank you for manifesting that reality by choosing to walk fearlessly and joyfully with me, into the healthy future that awaits us all.

ABOUT THE AUTHOR

Maria Barnes is a digital media professional whose work has taken her across the United States as well as to Europe, Asia, Africa, and the Persian Gulf. Her credits include cable and broadcast television series, an award-winning independent feature film, and hundreds of informational programs for government and private sector organizations. Her public television credits include producing a weekly public affairs series and editing a twenty-six-part PBS science series.

Barnes received a master of arts degree in film and video from the American University in Washington, DC. She earned a bachelor of arts degree in both International Studies and French from Miami University in Oxford, Ohio; and attended the University of Paris IV (La Sorbonne), where she earned a diploma of superior studies.

A senior member of Women in Film & Video (WIFV) and co-founder of the Television, Internet & Video Association (TIVA), Maria was an adjunct faculty member of both American

University and Northern Virginia Community College, where she taught video production. The author of *Put Cancer Behind You*, she lives in Fredericksburg, Virginia, with her husband and two dogs.

THANK YOU

Thank you so very much for reading. If you have questions about the topics I discussed in the book or would like to share your story with me, please feel free to connect with me.

Email: mbcprod@gmail.com
Facebook: https://www.facebook.com/maria.barnes.1000
Website: www.mariabarnes.net

Printed in the United States
by Baker & Taylor Publisher Services